From Hawera to Wigan

A life in Rugby League

Graeme West

with Andrew Quirke

London League Publications Ltd

From Hawera to Wigan

A life in Rugby League

© Graeme West and Andrew Quirke. Foreword © Bud Lisle.

The moral right of Graeme West and Andrew Quirke to be identified as the authors has been asserted.

Cover design © Stephen McCarthy.

Front cover: Playing for Wigan. Back cover: Coaching Wigan – winning all five trophies in 1995. Photo of Andrew Quirke by Alex Service. Background photo courtesy *Wigan Observer*.

All photographs in this book are from private collections unless otherwise credited. No copyright has been intentionally breached; please contact London League Publications Ltd if you believe there has been a breach of copyright.

A CIP catalogue record for this book is available from the British Library.

First published in Great Britain in November 2011 by:
London League Publications Ltd, P.O. Box 65784, London NW2 9NS

ISBN: 978-1903659-58-8

Cover design by: Stephen McCarthy Graphic Design
                    46, Clarence Road, London N15 5BB

Layout: Peter Lush

Printed and bound in Great Britain by Charlesworth Press, Wakefield

This book is dedicated to the game of rugby league. I've had so much out of it, I started playing for the love of it, it has given me so much pleasure in life.

Graeme West

Foreword

I am delighted to be able to write this foreword for Graeme's book. It has certainly been some time coming and I know that it is one that so many within rugby league are waiting to read.

He will not have to answer so many questions from the grandchildren on his sporting career, as they will have his book to read.

I have known Graeme for many years; I first came in contact with him when he was a tall teenager from Hawera playing for Taranaki Rugby League representative teams in the under-age tournaments. During that period I was either a New Zealand selector or a coach at those tournaments.

Later, when I was coaching the Wellington Rugby League Representative sides, Graeme was representing Taranaki along with Howie Tamati, Bruce Gall and the Christensen brothers to name but a few, coached by the very successful 'Sportie' Allen Marshall. They were one of the few teams to defeat Auckland on a number of occasions.

Having been deputy delegate for Taranaki Rugby League on NZRL Council to the late Ces Mountford MBE during this period, we had great relations with many fine players and administrators of Taranaki Rugby League. There were many great occasions in those days and to see Graeme get recognised for his achievements on-and-off the field makes one very proud.

He was selected for the Kiwis and they later played many test matches under his leadership.

He then went to England to play for Wigan, and he captained and then coached them; he won many trophies including the World Club Championship during that period.

Graeme, we know how close your family is, but I am looking forward to the day you decide to return to New Zealand. With our many discussions I believe you have much to offer rugby league in New Zealand.

I am so pleased that you have written your book and finally the full story is told! Congratulations Graeme, I hope the book goes well. I believe it will be very interesting with many highs and a few lows.

W.O. 'Bud' Lisle MNZM
Life Member New Zealand Rugby League

Bud Lisle has given a lifetime's service to rugby league in New Zealand. He played for the first New Zealand Schools team, in three trials to play for the Kiwis, against the 1958 British Lions and represented Canterbury, West Coast and Wellington at different levels. He was one of the people who initiated and organised the first Student Rugby League World Cup.

Dedications and thanks

I would like to thank Andrew for writing this book; we've had some great chats.

Graeme West

I would like to dedicate my work on this book to Oliver, with all my love.

Special thanks to Dani Bennett for her proofing skills.

Thanks to: Lindsey McCormick, Jacinta Hallows, Andy Hallows, Emily Quirke, Joyce Hallows, Walter Hallows, Garry Vaughan, Mike Appleton, Kate Wilkinson, Joanne Murphy, Ian Penketh, Caron Campbell, Alison Smith, Lisa Scully, Colette McKune, Richard Luck, Ben Smithurst, Chris Lawrence, Graham Wilson, Fiee Turner, Niccy Shiel, Chris Gill, Kev Gill, Mike Gill, Paul Gill, Mum, Paul Bennett, Mark Eccleston, Ste Radford, Andrew Langtree, Peter Lush and Dave Farrar, Roy Sloane, Ivy Hughes, Mike Critchley, Jack Gill, Joe Gill, Phil Wilkinson, Julia Ryan, Clayton Foster, Jennifer Patel, Greg Farrimond, Paul Kendrick. and The Masons Arms.

Most of all, I would like to thank Graeme West for the opportunity, it's been a pleasure and a privilege.

Apologies to anyone who I forgot.

Andrew Quirke

London League Publications Ltd would like to thank everyone who supplied photographs for the book, especially the *Wigan Observer*; Robert Gate for his help with research on Graeme's career in New Zealand; Steve McCarthy for designing the cover and the staff of Charlesworth Press for printing the book.

Bibliography

cherryandwhite.co.uk
Those who played by Bruce Montgomerie
The Kiwis – 100 years of International Rugby League by John Coffey and Bernie Wood
Various editions of the *Rothman's Rugby League Yearbook*
Various editions of the *Gillette Rugby League Yearbook*
Various editions of the *New Zealand Rugby League Annual*

Contents

1. **Early years** 1

2. **Switching to rugby league** 7

3. **International action** 21

4. **Joining Wigan** 29

5. **Beating the Australians** 41

6. **Winning the Challenge Cup** 53

7. **Player-coaching the 'A' team** 67

8. **Coaching Wigan** 79

9. **Super League ... and rugby union** 95

10. **Widnes** 103

11. **Motorways and Chorley** 111

12. **Developing players** 117

13. **Reflections** 133

Appendix: Statistics and records 138

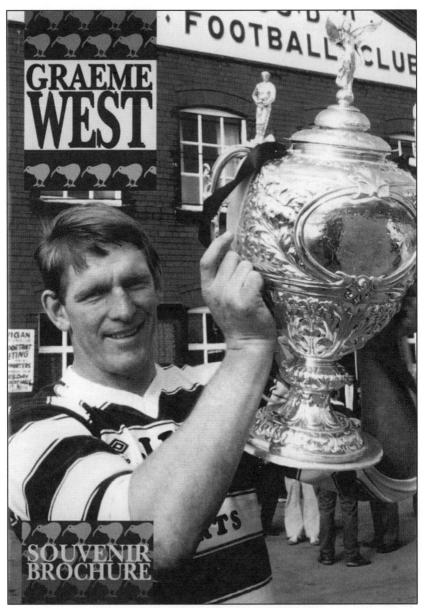

Graeme's testimonial brochure in 1993-94.

1. Early years

As a young boy growing up in the small town of Hawera in New Zealand, I would never have dreamed that I would end up not only travelling the world with my family as an international rugby league player, but I would also lift the famous Challenge Cup in front of almost 100,000 supporters at Wembley Stadium and then go on to coach one of the greatest club sides in the history of the game and beat the Australian champions in their own back yard to be World Club Champions.

It all happened though with more besides and it sometimes wasn't an easy ride. Here is my story...

* * * * *

In my family, when I was young on my mum's side there was only my grandfather. My grandmother died before I was born. They used to live in the King Country which is the middle part of the North Island, a very high, mountainous area of New Zealand. As kids we would go on the train to visit them once a year and it was a really good holiday. We would take a local train and then go onto the main line for a couple of hours which was a real experience. We used to look forward to it; we would stay a couple of weeks and then come back again.

It was a big holiday for us. Back in those days, people didn't have the money to travel far. It was really unheard of to go overseas on your holiday back then. It was a 150 mile trip to my grandfather's so it was a big deal to us as kids.

My mum's side of the family came from the UK. Her grandparents' name was Monroe and the family originally came from Scotland. Other parts of the family originated from Ireland, Denmark and Germany. My mum's maiden name was Remus.

My grandfather wasn't really into sport; he did a lot of market gardening and logging. A market garden is the relatively small-scale production of fruits, vegetables and flowers as cash crops, frequently sold directly to consumers and restaurants. He had an area of about four acres and kept a few sheep, he also had bulldozers and trucks. In those days, instead of square battens that you put on wire fences, he

1

used to split them and have rough battens. He would take his bulldozer into the bush and load up sledges with these battens. He was a tall man; I got my size from my mother's side of the family. He lived in a little area right on the main line called Rangataua. There were only about 400 people who lived there.

His house backed onto the bush. Behind the sheds with the bulldozers in was bush. We went exploring there. There was a garage where he used to do repairs on all his machines. We were into everything! We didn't go too far away though or we could have got lost.

On my dad's side, I never met my grandfather because he had died before I was born. My grandmother was still alive. They were a really rugby union orientated family. I have a great uncle who had been an All Black; Alfred Hubert West. He toured the British Isles with the 1924–25 rugby union 'Invincibles'. Listening to what people have told me, Alfred went to fight in the war and got gassed. He died quite young, just 40 years old; the effects of the gas had ravaged him.[1]

I have an uncle who has researched a lot of the family tree on that side of the family and it's interesting. My great uncle's brother was an elephant trainer. My uncle has produced a 40-page book on the pair of them; the All Black and the elephant trainer. He worked for Worths Circus. My mother has told me that we went to see that circus when I was a boy, but I can't remember it. He used to take the circus across the country on the train. The elephants helped unload things off the train. One particular day, he was sick and couldn't work so stayed in bed. The rest of the guys were trying to get the elephants to work, but no chance. They ended up having to rouse him out of his sick bed on a stretcher to give the orders to get the elephants to muck in.

My uncles were all into rugby union, my dad was mad about the sport. As a kid, I used to play union and I used to think the All Blacks forward Colin Meads was bloody marvellous. He was my hero and I wanted to be like Colin Meads. I used to have a chart on my wall each time the All Blacks toured that listed all the games. In those days, there was only the radio, to keep in touch with how the tour went on so I would listen to the radio then chart all the scores in my room.

---

[1] Alfred West made his test debut for the All Blacks on 27 August 1921 against South Africa. He won one more cap against the Springboks in that series, but did not play in the tests on the 1924–25 tour.

My mum's name was Shirley, my dad's name was Charlie and I was the eldest of four children, I have two brothers, Peter and Murray, and one sister Raewyn. My brother also played rugby league, he played for Taranaki second team. My sister was into netball and my youngest brother was into soccer or as they say in England; football, he played for the town so it was a real sporting family. My mum really supported all sports. A typical week for us would be Monday as a day off, Tuesday would be athletics, running the 100 metres and doing the long jump, Wednesday would be gymnastics, Thursday would be training for cricket, Friday would be rugby training and the weekends were for playing rugby. Every day we were involved with sport, we played basketball and volleyball too.

All our sports activities were helped by the house we had, by that I mean we had a big area at the back of the house where there was open land. It was 50 metres wide by about 400 metres long. All the kids used to go there and we had great times, playing war games and throwing mud at each other. It was great and it meant we had no time to get into trouble.

I come from Hawera, a town of 8,000 people, which was very spread out. There were very wide roads where there could be cars parked on either side, yet cars could still pass on either side. There was so much space a family could have a three bedroom bungalow with a double garage and a vegetable garden. It's completely different to Britain where there are so many people, meaning that land is precious. New Zealand is about the same land area as Britain, but there are only 4.1 million people living there. My town was based around dairy farming with some sheep farming. There were dairy farms all around the local towns and about 10 years before I left New Zealand, they had the biggest dairy factory in Australasia about a mile out of town.

My dad used to work in the dairy factory, he was head driver. In those days there were dairy factories dotted around the outskirts of the town. The small farmers transported their milk on tractors and other farm vehicles to the factory. My dad was based in the main factory and would take things to the smaller factories, such as coal for the boilers or he'd go and pick up cheese to take to the railway station. There was a fleet of three or four trucks and they would service all the local dairy factories. It was a logistics role. It was a very close community and if there was a bit of gossip, everybody knew.

New Plymouth was the main city in the region and was about 50 miles away; about 60,000 people lived there. Between Hawera and New Plymouth there was a mountain, at the bottom of the mountain by the sea was Hawera. The surrounding towns were all small communities based around dairy farming and the people were all sports mad. In a town of 8,000 people, Hawera had two rugby union clubs with teams at all age groups, from open age all the way down. There was also association football and also some rugby league, but that only existed at the junior level. They struggled to get going.

In Hawera, on a Saturday, mothers took their daughters to netball, there was an area of about eight netball courts and all the women were there. All the dads took their sons to rugby mostly but also soccer. Before lunch, they would watch the mothers play netball. After lunch, they would all watch the dads, brothers or uncles play rugby. At night the grandparents might mind the kids while their parents went out for a beer. There was also horse racing. Between taking their kids to sport, or playing sport themselves, the dads would find the time to place a bet at the TAB betting shop.

I remember when I got my first set of boots; because my feet were so big they could only find certain boots that would fit me. I used to hang them at the end of my bed. In rugby union, players had to use white laces so I would take the laces out of my boots and wash them. I would hang my shirt at the end of the bed too and could hardly wait for the morning to come so I could put it on and play. It was fantastic.

Rugby union at schools was based on players' weights, not ages. I was always big, tall and skinny, but still heavy with it. As a result, I always ended up playing with kids older than me. My dad said to me at one point, "You're not playing with them, they're too old for you." I told him, "If I've got to play with them to play the game, I'm playing with them." It was good for me because it gave me a grounding with older kids of my size. I wasn't running around with kids my age who were smaller than me, I would have just been able to run over them which would have made it easy. I had to do it the hard way. My dad was so into rugby, he went to all the games and be on the sideline; jumping up and down, screaming and carrying on.

I was about 14 years old when I was picked for the Taranaki provincial side, which is the bottom half of the province. However, by the time I was 16 I had become disillusioned with rugby union.

4

1970 Diamonds indoor basketball team, who won the Hawera and inter-town competitions. Back: C. Lawson, M. Davison (coach), D. Wills; centre: G. West, A. Nicholson, D. Weir, B. Thomas; front: H. Wills, S. Jenkins.

I was a second-rower jumping for the ball in the line out and giving it to the backs, they were having all the fun. As soon as the backs lost the ball, we would have to go and ruck for it and give it back to them again. I found that I got to run with the ball very rarely. I started thinking that I wasn't very sure about the game. I was also playing indoor basketball at the time and represented our town. I got picked in the Second Division New Zealand tournament team. I was doing alright. It was good to have hold of the ball and be involved.

As a kid, I went through the Cubs, Scouts and Air Training Corps. I always wanted go into the Air Force as the boss or one of the leaders. I was the same at Cubs, I always wanted to be one of the 'sixers' who led their own little group. I ended up being a Flight Sergeant in the Air Corps. It taught me a lot, we used to go camping with the leaders. It taught me how to take care of myself, cook meals and so on. One of the Air Training Corps officers was a national rugby league referee called Graham Church. He always used to give me a hard time, when I got my licence he told me I would lose it within six months. That really stuck to me and I thought, "I'll show you, you bastard". I always reminded him after that "I told you I'd keep my licence."

My mum had told me that I could leave school. "Thank Christ for that", I thought as I hadn't really enjoyed school. She had been to see the teachers to talk to them about me. She asked them how I was going to do and they said I wasn't so good at the exam side of things. Before I left school though, I sat the Chamber of Commerce exams in Maths and English, when the results came through I had passed them both. My mum was bloody ropeable [angry]! She went back down to the school and tore the teachers to bits. I told her I was finished with school though. I left to get a job in spare parts. I was only getting paid five or six dollars a week. There was a manager, a parts manager, a department manager and I was 'the boy'. A couple of staff left and I took on more responsibilities, but was not given any more money for it. I was getting pissed off. I had to do jobs outside of work to make ends meet. I delivered milk at four o clock in the morning then went to work then picked up hay bales after work. It was hard work, but it's alright when you're young.

I went to Fiji for 10 days with my basketball team and to make the trip I needed some cash. We did fundraising events and bottle drives. When I came back from Fiji, there was a big beef slaughterhouse opening in the town and there were rumours they would be paying big wages. I thought: "I'm having some of that". I went down to the slaughterhouse a couple of times to see the boss, but he told me: "You've got a job, you're alright." A mate of mine from school was his assistant. I went into my work and was told by the boss, "You're stocktaking this weekend, you've got to be in." I questioned this, then told him he could stick his job right up his rear end. He said, "You can't do that."

"I just did," I replied. I walked out straight to the slaughterhouse and told the boss, "Look I've got no job, he's sacked me." My mate urged the boss to give me a job and I was told I could start on Monday. I started washing the hooks and went on from there.

2. Switching to rugby league

I was still playing rugby union although I was pissed off with it. The boss of the slaughterhouse was a big rugby league man called Barry Giltrap. I had three real good mates at the slaughterhouse and one of them was playing rugby league. He said to me one day, "Come and have a game with us."

"I'm not playing that game," I told him. Rugby union was played all over the place in New Zealand while rugby league was only played here and there. My mate told me, "Look, we're going away for a pre- season trip, it will be a few beers and a stay overnight." I said, "I'm in for that."

We went away and he kept asking me to play, I told him I wouldn't be playing, but would watch. By half time, the side was getting beaten up, had three injuries and were losing. My mate told me they were short and I would have to play. "Alright then," I finally agreed. I put my boots on, scored two tries, we won the game and I bloody loved it.

I enjoyed the game, the way it was played, the way you could get hold of the ball and pass it. We had two rugby union teams in the town and my uncle was involved in one of them, I was supposed to follow in his footsteps. Fifteen miles out of town, there was this place called Stratford, which had a rugby league team. I thought, "Right, I'm going up there." I used to go up there to train and started playing rugby league. Eventually, a few of us got together and got a club going in Hawera.

My dad didn't say anything about me playing league, but I didn't see him watch me at games from that point onwards. He never went to a live rugby league game that I played in. He was rugby union through-and-through and a real stubborn bugger. That was a good thing because I gained something out of that from him. He was a hardworking man. In those days, it was six o'clock closing in the pubs. He would work his socks off all day and at half past four get on his push bike and burn rubber to the pub. He'd have an hour and a half of putting the beers down then jump on his bike to ride home. He'd have something to eat then be asleep in the chair. He loved a bet and loved his rugby union. He would also mow lawns or dig old people's gardens on a weekend just to make a few extra bob. He was a hell of a worker and that sort of rubbed off onto us. Both him and my mum would go and do extra jobs. They would give us kids an allowance, but we would go out and do extra jobs ourselves. We learnt straight away that if we worked, we could earn dough.

I would bag up pine cones and sell them to the neighbours for 50 pence a bag. I would also mow lawns and stack shelves in supermarkets and deliver milk and newspapers. I would do anything that I could to earn money. It set me right for later years.

Once I got going in rugby league people would tell me I was too long and skinny. I was six foot four inches tall by this point and only about 13 stones. I was told I would never make it and that only short, squat fellows could succeed in rugby league. I thought, "Right, well we'll see about that." Our team got going and I started doing alright and played for the town. I started playing rugby league around 1970 and remember the 1971 tourists that came to Great Britain and won the series. As a result, all my allegiance went to players such as Robert Orchard, Phillip Orchard and all the tourists as well as the Australian forward Arthur Beetson. New heroes.

The New Zealand Rugby League sent me a weight training programme. However, living in a town of 8,000 people, they didn't have gyms in those days. It was unheard of. One fellow called Brian Lithgow had a gym in his back garden. I was told he would let me use his gym, but would charge me. I would do my physically demanding job at the slaughterhouse, then go up the hill, turn right to go into his backyard and do weight training. Nobody had ever really done it before. I did it on my own, but it was part of what I had to do, if I wanted to do well, I had to do it.

All my mates seemed to be shortarses; they were all about five foot. My wife Maryann's brother is one of my best mates. There were four of us: Davy Lowe, a winger who played rugby league and got me into the game; Anthony Ropiha, known as Ducky, who is Maryann's brother; and a bloke called Billy Rowe who played rugby union. We all used to mate round together for three or four years while we worked for the same company, the beef slaughterhouse.

One day, we had unloaded a 100 tonnes of wheatmeal which they used to stack in a shed in sacks. They were in 120 pound bags and it was bloody hard work. We had to load them from the shed onto the truck. We really got stuck in and the boss told us he would pay us a full day's wages. We got the work done in half a day. The plan was to go across to the pub for a few beers. I went home first and sat down, next thing I was gone, zonked. I was absolutely stuffed. I had told my mum to wake me up around eight o'clock so I could go to the pub, which had a closing time of 10pm. She saw how tired I was and never woke me. I woke up around ten o'clock the next morning. I asked her why she hadn't woke me and she told me I looked "Bloody tired, but would be right now." It turned out that after a few beers, my three mates had jumped into a car, had an accident and one of them, Billy Rowe was killed. Billy and I had been planning to go to Australia. I thought, "What if I had been in that car?"

I kept being mates with the others and then I met Ducky's sister; Maryann. We got tied up and it went on from there. Those three mates had a big impact on my life. One got me into rugby league, one's tragic death stopped me from moving to Australia and the other one introduced me to my wife.

I got selected for my first provincial game; Taranaki versus Wellington. A lot of the players who had been on the Kiwis 1971–72 tour had come back from Great Britain and were playing for Wellington. Being from Taranaki, I was in awe of them, but I had been selected and I was playing. I went down there and we had a couple of really good props, one was known as 'Loopy' Lewis. He was little and short, but thick set. He unloaded me a ball during the game about 15 metres out and I scored by the posts. I just couldn't believe it. I came onto another ball and this time they were waiting for me. Boom! Down I went on my head. I got up really groggy. The trainer came on to me with water and I managed to keep going. At the end of the game, we had won it. It was a hell of a thing to do against heroes who I had up on my wall. I had not expected us to win.

I developed and went on to be selected for the North Island country team on three or four occasions. We played the touring Englishmen in 1975, we played the South Island and I played against the infamous Welshman, Jim Mills.

Around this time, I got married, we had my eldest son Vaughan and my daughter Toni; my youngest son Dwayne came later on. My wife Maryann loved the rugby and wanted to be a part of it. Wherever I went, she would jump into a car, bring the kids and come and watch me. If I was playing in Auckland, which was a five hour drive, she would throw the kids in the back of the car and she'd be away. They'd book into a motel somewhere or stay with family or friends all over the place. She was a big part of it. My mum was the same, she used to come as many games as she could. She was a big part of the committee in Hawera. She did a hell of a job there.

During 1974 and 1975 I was getting closer to being picked for the national side. I was told, "You're a country boy, only city boys get selected for the national team." I said, "Well, we'll see about that." I was selected in 1975 to tour Australia. I was told it was to be a learning tour for me, I was there to learn and that I may get a test at the end of the year in Britain.

We went on the tour and I did alright. We arrived at a game against a country side and I was told I might have to play blindside prop. I told the tour managers I had never played blindside prop before, but if I was selected I would give it a go. The match was at Seagulls, right on the border between Queensland and New South Wales. There was legal gambling on one side of the border so there was a little bridge with a sentry on over the river. People would go across the bridge, gamble and then come back. It was a beautiful place though with a big lagoon. I played blindside prop and scored a try. Later in the tour, I played second-row and again did alright. It was only a short tour of about five games with the international at the end which was a World Cup game. We got to the test and I was told I would be playing against Australia at blindside prop. I said, "Christ, I've only played there once in my life, but if you select me, I'll play, I'll give it a shot."

Anyway, I gave it a go against a side that had Graeme Langlands at full-back, Bobby Fulton at centre and so on. We ended up being beaten 36–8 and at the end of the game I managed to offload the ball for us to score. However, after that game, I was left in the wilderness on the international scene. From being told I was going on a learning curve, there was nothing for me until 1979. During that time, I went to every trial, I bashed up everybody I could, took up every ball, but still didn't get the nod.

What I found was in the local teams, players could organise what they needed to do. We knew what work needed to be done to get the end result. We knew each other's limitations and what everybody was good at. The end result was what mattered. What I found when I got to the New Zealand team was that the individual was what mattered.

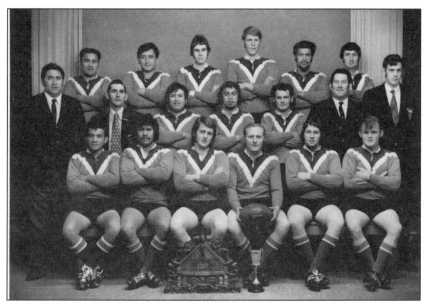

Stratford Rugby League senior team in 1971.

North Island country team that played Great Britain in 1974. Back: N. Aspin, E. Orchard, J. Tuineau, V. Snowball, K. Fisher, W. Rangi; Middle: T. Newton (coach), D. Raihe, G. West, G. Carlyon, W. O'Callaghan (manager); Front: J. Rutene, B. Berryman, W. Raihe, H. Waikai, P. Ravlich, R. Davies.

North Island representative team in 1976.

Graeme with his brothers Peter and Murray in 1975.

New Zealand international in 1975.

Everyone played for themselves and there wasn't a real big team plan. The players weren't really coordinated.

With the New Zealand team, I found that at test level I was trying to do everything, instead of being told what my specific job was. I tried to tackle everyone, take as much ball up as I could, support as many people as I could even though very often they were just going to die with the ball. I just blew myself away during some of those games. I thought, "If this is test rugby, I'm miles away from being fit enough." I was trying too hard and trying to do too much. It was just inexperience I think.

I remember the build up to games in 1974 against Great Britain. We had a coach called Tom Newton. He was really good. We would go up a few days before the game and he would train us bloody hard. It was far more organised. As a result, we got some reasonable results. It was easier for me to play.

I was doing well for Taranaki and became captain of the side. In 1979 the NZRL brought in the District series as another tier before the national level. There was now club, provincial, district – there were four districts in New Zealand – then the international side. The District series served as our version of State of Origin – well almost. It was good because the gap between provincial and test level was miles too big. It was like playing for Wigan St Pats then playing for the Lancashire amateur side then going to play a test match. Couple that with the lack of being able to organise a team properly and test rugby was real hard work.

Whenever Taranaki played Wellington, we always knew it was going to be a real ding-dong affair. I had often thought if we could get the majority of their backs with the majority of our forwards we would have one hell of a side and do some damage to someone. That's what the selectors for the district side did.

We always looked at Auckland, everybody would say they were this, they were that and were also a bit arrogant, the big city thing. The first district series we whomped them, we beat everybody. They were real tough games.

For one provincial game we went up to play Midlands, now they were all big fellows. They were islanders from Kinleith. They worked cutting down trees and were big physical blokes. The game kicked off and I took the ball in. One of these islanders kneed me in the back. I don't know if it was deliberate or accidental, but I do know that it hurt. I limped to the first scrum thinking it would run off. It was bloody killing me. It didn't get any easier so I had to go off. I looked at the player who had done it to me and thought "You bastard, whether you meant it or not you're having some". They had to come and play us at our place at the end of the season. I was ready to give him some. About a third of the way through the return fixture, he was in a tackle and his head popped up, I thought all my Christmases had come at once. Whack! I gave him a right rattler. He just looked at me and shook his head. "Oh no" I thought. I was getting ready to get out of the road fast. Barney Snowball, their full-back came through and yelled at him, "Cabbage, get on with the game." He got on with the game and I thought "Thank Christ for that". James Tenure, his name was, a big strong fellow. At the end of the game, we shook hands and had a bit of a laugh. I thanked Barney Snowball and explained that if it wasn't for him, I'd have been off behind the stand somewhere.

This same fellow and I played for North Island in 1974 against Great Britain at Huntley. Now James Tuineau had all the flashy stuff, the white boots, tape around his ears and so on. He looked the part. The British players started pulling his tape off and giving him a bit. He was bloody snorting, you could see the steam coming out of his nose. We gave him the ball on our 20 metre line, he went straight through the lot of them and scored under the posts. They were all lying spread-eagled on the ground shouting, "Tha ... mad, tha ... mad". We were just stood there cheering him, "Yeah!" He was like a raging bull.

The coach of the provincial side, Alan Marshall, was a real character. He had his specific rules. We had one training session a week because we already had one training session with our club each week. I arrived one week and he said there was to be a second training session later in the week. I asked him why he hadn't let me know earlier because I had something booked that I couldn't get out of. He told me if I didn't come to the other training session I wouldn't play. I told him again that I couldn't get there, but I had been to every other training session, despite being the player who had to travel the most. I had a 50 mile trip to make training.

I turned up on the Saturday as the team was getting ready to face Waikato. Alan named the team with me and another prop, Jim

O'Donnell, on the bench because the pair of us had missed the second training session.

There was a series of terraces on the side of the hill at this ground and we sat in the third terrace looking down on the game. After about 10 minutes Waikato scored. I could see Alan getting all tense and uncomfortable on the sidelines. A quarter of an hour later, they kicked another penalty to extend their lead. Alan started pulling at his shirt. Waikato kept up the pressure and the shout came from Alan, "Go on you c..ts, get out there". Jim and I went on and we ended up winning the game.

I remember a trial game where I did alright and was brought off before the end as they would do to a player if he had done well in a trial. Alan said to me, "Tell me, is Tupou out there?"

"Yeah, he's over in the corner," I replied.

"I couldn't see him, he's the invisible man. Every time I select him, I can't see him."

One time, Central Districts were to play Auckland, we hated them which was great for me motivationally. We were due to play them in New Plymouth in a new kit that hadn't arrived. The rest of the team were making a fuss about it. I told them to calm down, then asked if they would they go out and play Auckland in their underpants if they had to. I asked them to look at who they were playing against. I said if the kit turned up, fine, if not we would play them in our old kit and still beat them. They all said "Yeah". We went out and beat them. We knocked the stuffing out of them as well.

When we beat Auckland in that first district series, we were over the moon. We gave it to them because they were all up themselves. We had to beat South Island to win the series. They had players such as Mark Broadhurst and Alan Rushton playing for them, they were a really good side. It was a really close game. About 10 minutes into the second half, we had a second-rower called Bruce Gall who played for the Kiwis, a real tough, squat bloke from Inglewood, he took the ball up and Broadhurst smacked him. Gall's eye socket was badly injured in the challenge. His eye was all bloodshot. The referee stopped the game and gave Broadhurst a telling off. The ref looked at Bruce and told him he would have to go off.

"Fuck off," came the succinct reply. I told him he would have to go off because of his eye socket, but I got the same sort of answer. Bruce was adamant he was staying on. Now Broadhurst kept away from the ball for a while because he knew he was going to get some. Eventually, Broadhurst must have relaxed because he charged in with the ball. Bruce was waiting for him and kicking him in the bollocks. Broadhurst went down screaming and yelling. It bloody hurt me just looking at it. Bruce just turned to the referee and said, "Now I'll go off".

There was very good camaraderie between the players. When we went out in club games, we were all ready to give it to each other. When we played alongside each other in the provincial games, nobody picked on any of us, we all stuck together whatever happened. We once went right to the top of the North Island; we had an old bus and an old driver. It took us about eight hours to get there so it was a two night stay over. After the game, our manager, who was a young fellow called Stephen Riley and wasn't akin to all the ways of rugby players, was in the bar with us. We had won so we were having a few drinks. It was his first win as a manager so he got pissed. Stephen had a moustache that he loved and as he fell asleep at the bar, the players shaved half his 'mo' off. One of the players that night had been smoking cannabis and ended up at the police station. Stephen got a call to go down and sort things out. He knew he would have to go and have a bit of a wash before going down there and of course, when he looked in the mirror he was missing half a 'mo'. He had to shave the other half off before going down to the police station.

Willie Southern was one of the players I got on really well with; he was a big, strong Maori with a great family. We'd give each other hell on the pitch, but were great mates. The thing was, on the sidelines our kids would be doing exactly the same; they'd be playing rugby and generally be covered in mud from head-to-toe. We'd come off the pitch, get a shower then we'd go over to my mate's place. My kids would have a shower there and come back with all my mate's kids' clothes on. We'd have a beer and a laugh and say 'I'll get you next time' sort of thing. In the return fixture, we would give them their kids' clothes back. I wanted Willie in my team, but he could be lazy. I remember a training session we did with Alan Marshall where he wanted every player to run a certain distance in 12 minutes. If the player didn't manage it, he wouldn't be picked for the next game. Howie and I did it easily, but Willie was puffing around slowly. We thought "We need him in the team" so we went back and ran with him.

"I'm stopping, I can't do it, I'm knackered," he said.

"Get your arse into gear, you bastard," came the abusive reply to try and make him chase us.

He didn't make it; he ended up about half a lap short. Howie and I went to Alan and said: "At least we got him to do most of it, he's got to be in the side". Alan was having none of it at first, but we eventually managed to twist his arm enough to put Willie in the side. We used to call Willie 'Chocolate' because he'd always be eating the stuff before games. Whenever I went back to New Zealand, I always used to go and see Willie, catch up with him and have a great time. Sadly, he died of Leukaemia, when we go back now we visit his wife Francie and see how she is.

Another character was Willie's brother-in-law, Jack Knuckey, who was a half-back. He's the one who took care of my nose the first time. Knuckey had smashed my nose from one side of my face to the other. I was due to play basketball for my home town at a tournament in Hastings. I went to see a doctor who said, "You better not get another knock on it, it might stay like that". I thought he was kidding, but he insisted it could happen. I thought about it, but went and played anyway.

Jack used to play for the Waitara team. We played them at home one time and it was a really, feisty game. Knuckey was doing some damage to us in the game and in one tackle, his head popped up so I thought I'd give him some. As I went in to hit him his head flew back and smashed me right in the nose. It was spread all over my face. The first time you break your nose you end up with an Adam's apple the size of a tennis ball, it makes you feel sick. It wasn't his fault, he just got free from the tackle and his head caught me. Also, I was going in to hit him anyway. He was a good fellow to have around. He was big enough to play loose-forward but he was a good, tough, defensive half-back. He wasn't fantastic creatively, although he could do a job getting the ball around, but defensively he was very good. He knew all the tricks of the trade too. I got on really well with him.

One time, we went down to Wellington and it was the first time I had ever been in a sauna parlour. You could have a beer upstairs then downstairs you could have a Jacuzzi and a sauna. We didn't know it beforehand, but it was a mixed sauna. In the next sauna to us was a bloke with his beautiful girlfriend. Next thing, Jack sneaks past and gets in the sauna with them. When I went back to visit New Zealand I would always go and see Jack and his lovely family. Once I told him I was going to hire a car to go to Auckland and he volunteered to drive us there. He was also a scout for Canterbury Bankstown. When Canterbury came over to New Zealand, he would always go and join them, he loved all that sort of stuff. Sadly, around three or four years ago Jack died of cancer.

The older players used to show us the way. There was an old prop in Palmerston called Roy Roberts. He was slow, but he charged the ball up and if anyone happened to cross his path, he wouldn't go round the side of them, but over the top. He'd always warn everyone: "Don't come my way lad, you know what you're going to get."

I remember Kevin Tamati when we were due to play at Auckland in the District series. Auckland were saying how they were going to beat us and the headlines focussed on Vern Wilson who had been selected at prop to 'take care of' Tamati. Wilson was believed to be a bike gang member. I could see what was coming and spoke to Kevin. I told him "Don't even think about it. If we're going to win this game you need to stay on the park, if you start fighting, you'll end up on the sidelines."

"Piss off" he replied.

About quarter of an hour before half time, things started to get a little bit heated, trouble was going to start, so I grabbed Kevin telling him to get out of there. I turned around and the Auckland players all hit me. My jaw was killing me. At half time, we went into the changing rooms. I said to Kevin, "I told you not to get involved in fighting, my jaw is killing me."

"I told you to stay out of it," came his less than grateful reply. We ended up winning the game and afterwards I reminded Kevin, "I told you we needed you out there."

"Don't worry about me, I can handle myself," he growled.

I had to explain to him that I certainly wasn't worried about him handling himself, but I was worried about him being sat on the sidelines when we needed him out on the pitch.

In July and August 1979 New Zealand played Great Britain and I was selected as captain for the first test, which was a real honour. Some of the players in our side were playing in the Australian competition. We got a team thing together for the first time. Ces Mountford was the coach and he was a great coach. He'd gone round

New Zealand getting everybody playing and that's why Central Districts started to play well. He got people playing in a set way.

While playing for New Zealand in 1979, I took a bit of stick from the Auckland and Christchurch crowds. The country boys got a bit of that from the city people. I had captained Central Districts to win the District series and was put in as New Zealand captain. Perhaps it might have been better at that stage for me to have gone in as an ordinary player. I thought I'd go in and give it my best shot, but would admit I did not play exceptionally well. I was captain for the first two tests. We got beaten 16–8 and 22–7 and I didn't play so well. It wasn't a team thing, just in those two games I wasn't quite up to scratch. I was dropped for the third test and it was done in a way that really rankled Ces. He thought they should have stuck with me. After the second test we were in Christchurch. We were all in a bar having a beer when the selectors just came out and named the test side and I wasn't in it. They didn't pull me to one side or anything to tell me. Now Ces Mountford wasn't there, he was in a room upstairs. He sent a message down to me to go up and see him. I went up to see him and he was in tears. He was ropeable and told me: "I've had enough of this bloody lot, they can stick it."

I said, "Listen, don't even think about that, you keep your job, it's up to me to get into that team, I'm enjoying playing under you."

"But...", he started.

"No buts, stick with it, I'll get back in that team. I've been through it before, I've been told I'm not good enough."

The team went to the third test in Auckland, they played well and won, I was there supporting them.

There were some special people who gave me support in New Zealand and I'd like to thank them: Peter Leitch (the Mad Butcher), Ray Crance, Bud Lisle and Ray Coadie.

3. International action

The Kiwis were due to tour Great Britain in 1980 and there was another set of trials. I did well in them and was back in the squad to go on the tour. I came over to Great Britain and started to do well. I had gained more experience and was playing well. I had a bit of an injury just before we left that I never told anyone about, I just thought "I hope it comes right." We had a great tour with some great wins.

It was the first time I had come over to Great Britain. I loved touring; it was bloody brilliant coming away with your mates. We had a great time. We stayed at Blackpool for a week at first, training. Then we played the Blackpool side as a warm up. I didn't play in that game, but the next game was against Hull at Boothferry Park. It was absolutely jam-packed with 15,945 in the Hull City football ground. We beat them 33–10 and it was an incredible experience looking round to see so many spectators and how much noise they made. Back in New Zealand, I was used to playing in front of about 100 people. We just used to play for the enjoyment which they did in Great Britain too, but they also got big crowds and they got paid for it as well. I played back home and never got paid a bloody scorrick. I had to do all the meat raffles on a Friday night to keep the club afloat, then pay five dollars to get on the minibus on a Sunday to travel to our away games. It was another five dollars if I wanted to take my son to the game. Then I'd play in the game, knocking each other about, then pay another three dollars for a meal afterwards. It was the same in Australia, they did get some decent crowds, but nothing like in Great Britain. I just thought to myself, "I'd love to come over here and play."

I had a great tour. We drew the first test at Wigan 14–14 and won the next at Bradford 12–8. Then there was the final test at Leeds. We didn't play so well, but we felt that we were never going to win that game. We hardly seemed to get a penalty all afternoon and lost 10–2.

They were really rough games too; also, they had a different way of scrummaging in England. Back home, our scrums were straighter. In England, the hookers were out of the tunnel and so on. We were based in Harrogate and we did a lot of scrum training. The shout was, "tighten the scrum up", my ears ended up bleeding because the scrums were so tight. We competed though. We drew the test series and won most of the big games.

21

The 1980 New Zealand tourists. (Courtesy *Rugby League Journal*)

We had a game in London at Fulham FC's Craven Cottage, where Fulham RLFC had just started. We played against the Great Britain under–24s and beat them 18–14. I remember being on the streets of London looking up at both sides at the tall buildings, it was like a concrete jungle. It was cold too, I thought "What a bloody awful place, bloody rubbish".

We went to France and it was the same, bloody freezing. One game we played on a Friday night and there was sleet and snow during the game. After the game, our showers were cold too. "What the hell's this," we thought. So we looked down the line and all the French players had the hot water. We all headed down to that end and the French players were given no choice but to move aside.

On the Sunday, we played on a frozen ground. It wasn't flat either; there were chunks out of the pitch where they had been playing on it. We didn't know any better, we just played. We never, ever had a frozen ground back in New Zealand. The hardest grounds I was used to playing on were in Australia where they were baked hard with the sun. We played anyway and it was hard work with players slipping all over the place. One of their players made a charge down the wing, he looked like he was going to score and I gave chase. I weighed up whether I was going to dive on the rock hard surface, "Shall I or shan't

22

I," I thought before bringing him down. My knees were red raw as a result.

Some of the French referees were unbelievable; we thought that the referee that day gave them everything. He stood in the middle of the scrum rattling on in French; we didn't have a clue what he was talking about. We all got pissed off with it. That day we had Mark Broadhurst and Howie Tamati in the front row and they packed down on him. They got up and he wasn't happy about it. We managed to win that game.

We got to the tests. The rule back then was that you fed the scrum if you were at your end of the field. If you had made a mistake, you would put the ball in, but they would have the head. This ref let them put the ball in the scrum at both ends of the park. The French won the first test 6–5 and we were mad at the referee, we wanted to kill him. In those days, there were no handovers on the sixth tackle, so teams relied on winning the scrum to get the ball. We had no chance. After the game, as per usual, the French were all sticking together. The referee was right in the middle of them in the room we were all in. The French knew that if the referee went back to the dressing sheds he was going to get a kick in the bollocks. He stood there, sipped his drink and looked around, he knew something was up. He went out with the mob, out to their cars and away they went. I thought "If I see him again, he's going to get it," but it never happened.

We won the second test 11–3. It was a tough game, but the referee was a bit fairer. A drawn series probably suited the French; they knew they weren't good enough to win a series against us.

What I found over there was that the French treated us like muck. We'd be staying at a place and they'd make us travel 40 miles to a training session. I thought "What a bloody awful place this is." Looking back, I've since been back to both places; London and the south of France and I loved them. What it has taught me is that before you make a decision on something; give it a bit of time. When people get older, they realise it's not just about the bad weather or the bad areas. Even in the bad weather, some of the places are pretty good. When the weather's good, it's better still.

We went to a hotel in France and it still had the bullet holes in from the Second World War. There was an alleyway down the side of the hotel, there were stone buildings on either side, when mopeds went down it, they made a hell of a noise. I was sitting in the bath one day and I heard a moped rattling down the alleyway, I then heard a 'whoosh' and a 'put-put-put' noise. The next thing, a player came into my bathroom with an empty rubbish bin, scooped up some water from my bath and gave the moped rider another one.

Another rule on tour would be that the player who ended up in the front in a taxi had to pay; there were desperate battles between players trying to squeeze their shoulders into the back. The taxi driver would be going mad because his taxi would end up a foot wider than it was when he picked us up.

We went back to New Zealand at the end of the tour. Then I played for Central Districts in Australia in April and May 1981. We had won the District series and for that we got a shot at the Tooth Cup. That was a midweek competition in Australia.[2] We played Manly and Penrith. The Australian standard of play was too high for us at that point. It took a while to get used to it. We went over to Australia and gave it a shot, but we just weren't used to playing at that level.

Our manager brought a psychologist in. He was a big, fat fellow who came in and had about four of our pre-game meals. He told us to lie down on the carpet as the manager said, "Yes, this is good for you".

"Are you sure?" we asked.

We lay down on the carpet as he told us we were all asleep and when we went out on the pitch, we were going to be fantastic. We were all looking at each other thinking "What the hell's going on here?" We thought it was just bullshit basically.

In June the French came over to play us. I had two good tests against them. I set up some tries in one of the tests. The crowd started warming to me a little then, but not greatly. Part of the problem was still the city-country thing. The New Zealand team had previously been made up of predominantly Auckland based players. It wasn't until Ces Mountford came in as coach and went around the whole country that talent from elsewhere was used. He would pick the best players out of every province. Most of the talent that he selected would later be bought by overseas clubs in the mid–1980s. There was me, Howie Tamati, Kevin Tamati, Mark Broadhurst, Gordon Smith and Gary Prohm. Gary was from Auckland, but was still a good player.

---

[2] The competition had various sponsors over the years, and in 1980 and 1981 was sponsored by a brewery, Tooth & Co.

In 1982 I was named as captain for the tour of Australia and Papua New Guinea. I had roomed with Mark Graham previously throughout our tour of Great Britain; he was a good player and a nice fellow. He was playing in Australia at the time for Norths. He captained the test side. I was tour captain for the other games because Mark only came in the week before the tests. He would then go back to playing for Norths. I understood that at the start of the tour and was fine with it. We discussed it and there was no problem, especially as he had more experience than me of playing professionally.

In the first test on 3 July we were winning 8–6 with about five minutes to go. It was a really tough contest. Muggleton came on and scored a try for them and Cronin kicked the conversion off the touchline. We lost 11–8 and I was totally pissed off. It had been a very tough match, I got my eye split. During the game, Rohan Hancock came charging through and Kevin put him on the deck with a shoulder charge. They had to throw water on Hancock to revive him; he kept away from Kevin after that. The interesting thing after the game was that the newspapers reported that "Hancock moves up to front row to take on Tamati in second test". I shook my head because I knew that would be like a red rag to a bull for Kevin. Lo and behold, an early scrum in that second test and Kevin hit Hancock without reply. We could just see Hancock sinking. He was out and had to be revived again.

In Brisbane we were all as sore as hell. There was a New Zealand fellow living in Brisbane, a bit of a wheeler-dealer who wanted to be a part of things while we were on tour. He told us he could get us a spa. We thought that was great because the grounds were hard and we had been knocked around a bit. We went into the place and there was a spa pool on one side with a bar on the other. It was a big, posh place. We thought this was great so went to get changed and came back out. Next thing, all these ladies came out. It was a brothel.

"Hey, hey," I shouted at him. "Where have you brought us?"

We all left quickly because I could imagine the headlines in the following day's papers.

Howie and Kevin Tamati used to give players nicknames in the New Zealand side. There was Billy Kells the winger, he used to win all the cash in the card games. They used to call him 'Billy Big Pockets' because his pockets would hang down with all the money that was inside them. If the camera was there, Howie and Kevin would be there, they loved it. We nicknamed them 'long light' and 'flash light'.

During the tour, the players who didn't play in the tests would play in the midweek games and if any of them were playing particularly well they could force their way into the test side. The problem was the midweek side went off the rails. Some of them were playing badly, some were going out. We had to bring them in and discipline them.

We went to New South Wales and played the country champions Riverina. We had a team meeting beforehand and the message went out, "Right, nobody goes out tonight". We needed to get the tour back on track and to make sure there was a crowd for the test at Sydney. It should have been the midweek side playing, but we pretty much played our test team.

So the players who usually played in the midweek team had to stay in, and didn't get a game. They were all mumbling and moaning about it. The tour manager came out and said we could all collect our tickets for the midweek game. Everybody got in line until one player got to the front and said, "I don't want your bloody tickets, stick 'em" to the manager's face. Now Kevin was about three behind him in the queue and I was directly behind Kevin. Another player got his tickets when he came storming back in, "Yeah I'll take the bloody tickets" because somebody must have said they would have his off him. Tamati said, "No you won't" and gave him a slap. "Well done," I said. He deserved every bit of it.

We went out and won the game quite convincingly which helped us get things back on track.

The tour went on and the midweek side still weren't playing well, they were getting a bit unruly. We then played the second test which we lost 20–2 at Sydney Cricket Ground. We made a couple of mistakes in the game that the Australians capitalised on.

Off we went to Papua New Guinea and played one test up there. That was a hell of a place, quite unusual for us. We arrived at Port Moresby to watch a local game. We were sitting in the stand and noticed massive wire fences around the ground. There was an altercation on the pitch, all of a sudden, spectators appeared from out of bushes and through the wire fences. "This is a wild place" I thought as we all went back to the hotel talking about it.

We flew to Garoka in the Highlands where we stayed in a teacher's compound. The beds were only about five foot long so I had to put my feet on a table at the end of the bed. It's all part of the experience, the players had to make do. I played in that game. I noticed that there were two strands of wire across each side of the field. The referee wasn't helping us, but it was a pretty tough game anyway. It was a very close game. One of their players smacked Shane Varley, our half-back and they scored soon after. We got together behind our line, some players were saying, "Let's go down and smack the bastards, let's give it to them."

I said, "Look at the sidelines." You would have to have been there to believe it, but people had come out of the bush, they had war paint on and were holding spears. They were in the trees and everything, all round the place. It was unbelievable. I said, "If you want to go and smack them, you do that but I'm going to get on with playing the game." There was a distinct possibility that this could end in a riot and if they had spears, I didn't want one stuck into me. We won the game. When the ref blew the whistle, all the spectators came onto the pitch. Suddenly, my leg was over one of the spectator's shoulders as they were attempting to chair me off. They were all trying to touch us and slap us on the back. They are all short fellows over there and with my height, they must have wondered where I had come from. It was quite an amazing thing. Two of my mates weren't playing in this game and were watching from the top of the stand, they were laughing, I was crapping myself. We managed to get out of it alright though.

Some parts of Papua New Guinea were like paradise. I remember the programme *Fantasy Island* – 'da plane boss, da plane'. Well we came in on this small plane, there was a big lagoon with a little island in the middle of it. We came into land and it was a fantastic place. There was an Aussie and a New Zealander there, one had a boat, one had a car. They let us borrow the car for a trip around which was great. They said they would take us to the lagoon to see the dolphins. We ended up in the water with dolphins jumping up around us, it was amazing. We walked into the bush and we could see where the Japanese had been during the war and the tunnels they had made.

The Aussie who had the boat told us on this particular day that those of us who weren't playing could come out with him for a trip. Now one thing I had always wanted to do was to go on a deserted island by myself. Three of my mates came with me on this bloke's boat. I asked the bloke if he could drop me off on the little island, it was probably only about as big as a local pub. He dropped me off there with half a dozen beers and my hat on. I just lay under the palm trees while those silly buggers were going up and down fishing. They got sunburned to death. I reminded them before they left me, "Just don't forget to pick me up."

We won the test match over there 56–5. It was quite strange, I would take the ball up and always be able to offload up top due to the height difference. Our player would score, but their players wouldn't be worried about where the ball was, they just wanted to get me. About four of them pile-drove me into the ground. If they had the right physical stature, they would be a hell of a side. They were very physical, aggressive and had some skill too. I watched the Anzac test between Australia and New Zealand in 2011 and I noticed that there are more people from an ethnic minority background playing the game now. They've got some great skills. If Papua New Guinea players were just a foot taller, they would be exactly the same. It's like the Japanese in rugby union, they are good players, just not physically big enough.

I was given the supporters' player-of-the-tour award.

4. Joining Wigan

After that tour, I got offers to go and play for Canberra and Illawarra. They were two new clubs that were starting out, they told me what they could offer me. I explained to them that as a beef slaughterman I was getting paid around $1,000 a week. That was 35 years ago, and was a lot of money. I told both clubs that I couldn't leave my job for what I was being offered, but that I would at least consider it. I went back to work and Wigan had rung up. Ces Mountford, who had been a Wigan great in the 1940s and 1950s, told me that Wigan had been in contact, he had been speaking to Jack Hilton, one of their directors, about me and they wanted me there.

I got the New Zealand player-of-the-year award and had to go to the presentation. While I was there, Wigan rung up. I asked them what they had to offer and again, it was less than what I was earning in New Zealand. I said, "It doesn't matter, I've had enough. I've done all I can do in New Zealand." I had enjoyed playing in the tour games in Great Britain in front of the big crowds. When we had toured Great Britain in 1980, Wigan were in the Second Division and we didn't play them. They invited us to Wigan though to do a presentation for Ces. He told me, "If this place ever gets off the ground again, it's a sleeping giant." I remember that afternoon, a few of the players walked into Wigan town centre. I wanted something with Wigan on it as a souvenir because I had heard so much about Wigan rugby league. I was after a jersey or something. I went into a sports shop in the middle of town and there was bugger all. I thought that was unusual for a rugby league town that had such a big name in the game. I found a box in the corner and pulled out a scarf that was red and had 'Wigan' on it. The other half of the scarf was blue and had 'Athletic' on it, I thought it must be an amateur team.

As there was nothing else, I bought it and took it home. It wasn't until I came back over to the UK in 1982 that I realised I had taken a football scarf home. I suppose if one of the Wigan Athletic supporters had seen me wearing it round my neck at the time, they'd have laughed like hell.

Ces had told me that some of the local clubs in the area had some marvellous games and rivalries with Wigan. He told me about some of the games he had been involved in and the type of crowds which had attended. I always marvelled at the attendance at the Halifax versus Warrington Challenge Cup Final replay in 1954 at Odsal when there had been over 100,000 people there. Ces was Warrington coach at the time and to hear him tell me there were fences pushed over by the crowd and so on was amazing.

So, I knew what Wigan was about and knew about the crowds over in Great Britain so I said to the missus, "What do you reckon? I'm up for it."

She said, "Right, we'll go then."

Within two weeks, we had sold the car, rented the house out, sold the furniture and given away everything we didn't want to keep and we were away. I had toured the world and the idea of going to England was so that my family could tour the world too. My wife and kids had stayed home while I had been on tours, now I wanted to take them off to show them the world.

I had been told by Wigan that when I came over I would have the choice of two houses and three jobs. My wage with the club would be £7,500 a year. I said that would be fine. Wigan also had to pay the New Zealand Rugby League $40,000 because of my amateur status. Ces had introduced that fee for professional clubs to assist with funding the continued development of the game over there. That money would go back into the pot to develop the next generation of players so it was a good idea. New Zealand had put their time into developing me and wanted to be compensated for that.

We were told that our work permits would be at the airport when we arrived and we jumped onto the plane. The kids were only aged nine, seven and two at the time. I thought because it was a long journey it was better to stop off at Singapore. We did that and then it was a 12 hour flight to London. I had spent some money on a video recorder and didn't have much money on me. I didn't think that would matter because when we arrived, we would go straight through anyway. We got to Heathrow and the following exchange took place:

"Where are you going sir?"

"I'm going to Wigan. I've come to play rugby league, there should be a work permit here for me."

"There's no work permit here sir. Just give us a bit of time, who can we get in touch with?"

"You'd better get in touch with Wigan Rugby League".

So we stayed in the holding area, the kids were knackered at this point after 12 hours on the plane. We sat down for a while and I got the kids a drink. I wanted to get them all a meal but I didn't have any money. The banks had closed and there was no such thing as a hole in the wall back then. My wife said, "Go and do something about it, I've had enough of this."

I went back to the desk and said, "I'll give you a deal. Let me through as I have a family here that needs to be fed or I will go through anyway."

He said, "You can't do that sir."

"You just bloody watch me," I replied.

At this point, Danny Campbell from Wigan had arrived and they told me they could let him through but not let me out. I said that was ok. Danny came through and sorted it all out for us. Four hours later, they let us through. So, that was 16 hours, and then came a four hour railway trip up north. The missus was jumping up and down about it all, but sometimes you've got to roll with the punches. I just thought, "Well I've signed to come here, I'm not turning around to go back."

We got to the station and were staying at the Bellingham Hotel in Wigan. We got the kids hunkered down and then a message came up that Alex Murphy was at the hotel and wanted to see me. I went down to the bar and Alex was there with the football manager Larry Lloyd. They welcomed me and I said, "Look, I've been on the go for 20 hours, I'll have a quick beer and I'm off."

As I had just come off a New Zealand tour, my boots were stuffed, my trainers were stuffed so I had just thrown them away. I thought "I'm going to a professional club, they will have access to everything I need there." When I got to Wigan, they had nothing for me partly due to the size of my feet. The first two training sessions I had to do in my socks. We were training at Rose Bridge High School and when we went outside, it was raining and I was slipping all over the place. When we trained on the tarmac, it wore the soles out of my socks. They were trying to get boots for me to play in from Walsh's in Bolton. They managed to get me a pair to play in for my first game. My trainers followed a week later.

When I first came to Wigan in the early 1980s, things were bad. There weren't many jobs around, the house prices were down. They think things are bad today, it was bad back then. It got on its feet in the late 1980s and early 1990s and there have been ups and downs since then. Life goes on through the peaks and troughs. Whoever comes up with the system where things are good all the time will be a rich man, it never happens. In your own life, things aren't always peaches and cream. When a down comes, you've got to treat it as a challenge.

The town itself though was all small alleyways. A mate of mine had told me before we came across that everybody lived on top of each other and that there would be people calling round for a cup of sugar and so on. The fellow at the Bellingham Hotel, Roy Thomas, was marvellous with us, and tried to do as much as he could to get things right for us. It was tough on the kids though, they weren't used to being freezing cold outside and boiling hot inside the hotel. They were jumping around and causing mayhem. The missus said, "We can't bloody stay here, the kids will go bananas". We ended up at the hotel for six weeks. After the second week, I went down to the club and asked, "Where's this bloody house and where's this job?"

"Ah, er, we'll have to see about that," came the reply.

"You told me they were ready to go" I said.

"Er, ah, well, no," they said.

After about five weeks, they took us to a house and there was nothing in there, it was just a shell. There was no light fittings, no sink. There was bugger all in there. The missus said, "We are not staying in here."

"I don't blame you," I replied.

Roy Thomas said to me, "I know where there's a place in Winstanley if you want to have a look at it." He took me up there and it was a nice place which I thought would suit us. We moved in, it was near where George Fairbairn used to live. We had a house now.

I'm a taxi driver now and recently I was at Wigan station and I saw this fellow looking around, he came up to me and said, "My mobile phone's gone dead, can you lend me your mobile phone?"

"Roy, for you anything," I replied.

"Thank you very much lad," he said. "Who are you?"

"Graeme West." He was delighted to see me again. "The way you looked after us Roy, you can have the bloody car if you want, I'll take you anywhere you want to go."

So, we moved into a semi-detached house in Winstanley. One night, at around seven o'clock, the kids had a party. I was at training at the time and the fellow from next door had come round moaning about the noise. I got in about half eight and said I would go and see him. My wife told me that I shouldn't go anywhere near him. I thought I'd better stay away.

The kids all got mates, their families took them under their wing. It was great with them not having uncles, aunties and grandparents here. Each of our kids got a mate whose house they would go round and stay at. They used to go on holiday with them. My eldest son Vaughan had a mate called Neil Molyneux, his mum and dad were called Pat and Ronnie. Sadly, Pat passed away, but Ronnie is still a really good friend of mine. He acts as a sort of uncle to Vaughan.

It's the same with my daughter Toni; her mate was Hannah Watson, her mum and dad were Jude and Dave. Toni and Hannah used to go everywhere together, in fact Hannah even came to New Zealand with us on one of the tours.

Dwayne, my youngest, had a good mate in Kenny Hewitt. His mum and dad were Rita and Dave. Dave's one of my best mates and I enjoy going out having a beer with him.

Joyce, next door has been living there all the time we have been there. Her husband, Bill Maltby, used to be the driver for the Mayor. I got on really well with him. He always took the Mayor to London when Wigan went to Wembley. Bill would be in the do after the game and I talked to him more than anybody else. He passed away 10 years ago. Joyce has been like another mum; I go over and have a chat with her. The past two winters were that bad that my kids have gone over to clear the snow for her and see that she's alright. I always have a laugh with her. She comes over to order a taxi and insists that she'll pay, but I never let her, and explain that she's done enough for us.

All of these people were like another family to us.

Wigan were paying me £150 a week and we couldn't really live on it. I chased them again about the job I had been promised. The club video man came in; Derek Hitchen, a nice fellow. He said, "I've been told to drive round with you to see if we can find you a job". We went to two or three places, including a slaughterhouse, but there was nothing doing. We went out to Atherton and a man called Barry Holmes said, "I can give you a job, but you'd have to be here to start around half seven or eight o clock each morning."

To get to Atherton from Winstanley, I had to get a bus at six o' clock in the morning to take me into Wigan, then another bus to take me to Atherton. When I came in at night, I'd grab my gear and go straight to training. When I got back from training, my kids would be in bed. In the morning, I would be gone before they got up so I wouldn't get to see them unless I had a night when there was no training. I just had to put up with it. I always thought that if I was going to make a go of it, I couldn't go back home. Nobody back in New Zealand was going to tell me I couldn't handle it. I was going to put up with whatever was necessary to get on with it. Of course, I would say my piece along the way.

The job in Atherton was for a wholesale butcher, selling meat to the bakeries. I just went round trying to get new orders. I had a book with a map and away I went. There was one time I was trying to find a pie manufacturing place. The bloody map said it was right in front of me, but all I could see was a new housing estate. It took me about 45 minutes to find a path that led to the place.

I loved the local accent, dialect and expressions of the people I met when I came over. I used to sit in a pub and just listen to the old blokes, "Tha knows" and so on. It was one of the highlights listening to how they spoke. I got two fellows in the cab recently just after last orders. One of them got in with a: "Can thee tek us to Higher Ince?"

"Yeah, no problem," as we waited for his mate to get to the cab.

"E'll be ere soon, ee's been awht."

His mate jumps in the back.

"Wha's been? Wha's been?"

"Ar've been awht back thur."

"Ar've been lookin' for thee."

"Ar've been awht 'avin a smook."

That's part of the experience and it's bloody brilliant. It amazes me the number of people I talk to who have a downer on Britain as a place to live. They can be young or old and they pick up on my accent and ask me, "What are you doing in this dump?"

I tell them that I've been all over the world and Britain is no dump, it's a great place. There are the facilities for people to get educated and you can go wherever you want to go in the world if you have the drive. Some people just expect to go out into their back yard and pick £10 notes off the tree. They all want something for nothing. We all expect a reasonable shot at success in life, but you have to work for it. You've got to get the best out of what you got.

Wigan is in a great spot, on either side are Liverpool and Manchester and it is possible to get a train straight to Edinburgh or London. Then there's the Lake District, the airport and the sea. I'd never call my home town or New Zealand a bad place. I love it to bits and I like here too. The only thing I don't like is the winter.

I was getting a bit pissed off with the travel to and from work so I said to Maurice Lindsay, "Look, I need some transport". With all the expenses I had incurred, I didn't have the dough to buy a car myself. He told me he thought he could get me a car. I went down to the club and they had a Hillman Avenger for me. Maurice told me: "You'll have to keep filling the radiator up, it's got a hole in it." So, I would fill it up each day and take it to work. At the end of the week, Maurice told me: "Someone wants to buy the car, you'll have to bring it back." I was back on the buses again.

The local Wigan paper put a photograph of me with an animal carcass over my shoulders, playing on my former job as a slaughterman. They also couldn't get over how big my feet were. They had me sit on the couch with my feet up so they could take a picture.

Wigan had only been promoted back to the First Division the year before I came to the club. When I first arrived, I think they were still trying to work out who was a director and who wasn't. Four were really trying to take the club forward, but you would find old directors turning up on the coach for away games too. They were convinced that Alex Murphy was the darling of everybody and was the man to take the club forward.

During this time, I was finding out what Murphy was like. He must have been a great player in his time from what everybody says. As a player-coach he must have been brilliant, but as a coach I thought that there was too much running in training and not enough ball work. He'd come in and say, "Run it". I would say, "For Christ's sake, we've gone back to how it was when I first started playing in test matches". I thought that there was no structure and no team work on how to play together. It made it so difficult; I thought we needed to work on our team work as a defensive unit and team work as an attacking side with planned moves. We were all doing individual stuff. I was getting pissed off with it so started jumping up and down about it a bit.

My first game for Wigan was at Leeds on 21 November 1982. Mick Scott was one prop and Lee Bamber was the other. Leeds got the better of us, but my main memory is of the snow coming horizontally across the scoreboard. I thought "What am I doing here". I ended the match freezing cold and then experienced that uncanny feeling of getting into a hot bath when I was ice cold. I just thought I had to get on with it.

My first game at Central Park was a 45–0 win over Featherstone Rovers on 26 November. Everything just fell into place for me and I scored two tries. It was a freezing Friday night and the pitch was very firm. Once I got warm though, it was brilliant conditions to play in. Everybody had come together and I could tell there was a lot of potential there. I was very surprised to read the next morning that the Featherstone coach had been sacked. It made me think that they did things dramatically in Britain.

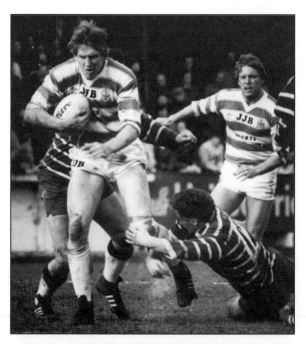

First try for Wigan – against Featherstone Rovers
at Central Park in November 1982.

I am tall so I could be tackled and unload the ball over the top. As games went on and we got of a bit of a roll on, some of the other players were playing better than they previously had.

I always thought that after the game, the players would go and have a beer. We had worked hard throughout the week. During Murphy's time he would tell us we weren't allowed to drink. I used to think "Get stuffed, I've worked hard this week" and I would go for a beer anyway.

Between the 'A' team dressing room and the first team dressing room there used to be the big plunge pool where there was a communal bath after the game. They did away with that because of blood getting in the water and so on. The other side of the plunge pool was the sauna. Alex Murphy used to love the sauna at the club. He must have done something to somebody as one day, because as soon as we came in, the smell hit us. Murphy came in and went to get in the sauna to discover that somebody had pissed on the stones. He went bananas.

Nicky Kiss was a pearler, he had a lot of tenacity. He had a lot of ability too. In those days, the hooker could pinch the ball in the scrum. If we were under the cosh in a game and Nicky came up with the ball, everybody would be smiling. He was like a small bear, if he had been a big fellow he'd have been bloody dangerous. I remember before a game at Whitehaven, when we were getting ready Nicky would have this habit of cracking other players across the chest and shouting, "Come on!" This one day at Whitehaven, I wasn't expecting it and he nearly sent me flying. "Piss off you stupid bastard," I told him. Everything about Nicky went towards his performance and his game, he was great. He could irritate people at times, but could also lift them. He reminded me of the cartoon character 'The Tasmanian Devil'.

Brian Case was another really solid player. He would cart that ball up all day and was a great number 10. Other players always wanted that sort of player in their side. Andy Platt was another of that ilk as were Dane Sorenson and Kevin Tamati. A number eight is usually a fellow who does a bit of ball playing. A number 10 is the player who, when everything is breaking down, would charge the ball forward. Their job is to steady everything. That was Brian to a 't' and he was an integral part of the side then. People say that the forwards build the platform and the backs work off it and there's a lot of truth in that.

Lord Derby being introduced to Graeme before the 1983 John Player Trophy final against Leeds at Elland Road. (Courtesy *Wigan Observer*)

We won the John Player Trophy in January 1983 although to be honest I didn't have a good game. I got replaced after half time and the side went on to win. That was good because I knew I hadn't played so well. One of the funny things about the day was after I had been replaced I was sitting outside the dugout feeling a little bit sorry for myself thinking "You can do better that that". Wigan scored, Murphy came out from the side of the dugout and yells to me, "Get that fucking sand out there will you". I thought, "Who's he fucking talking to?" He again yelled, "You". I grabbed the sand and took it on to Colin Whitfield who was kicking. I told Colin, "Make sure you kick it mate". I came back with the bucket of sand and Murphy was sat next to Bill Ashurst in the dugout. I went to throw the sand over Murphy, but pulled back at the last minute because he ducked behind Bill.

I got on really well with Bill. He said to me after the game, "Jesus, Westy, I thought you were going to let me have it."

I told him, "When he ducked behind you, I thought better of it. If he'd have stayed where he was, he'd have got it right in the mouth."

When I first came over to Britain, I used to get a lot of stick from some British players for "taking our money". I would just give them a bit of stick back and as time went on, I earned opposing players' respect. There was one incident when Howie Tamati first arrived, he came over a few months later than me. We were playing in Yorkshire and one of the opposition's props came charging through. Howie picked him up and dumped him on his head. The prop got up and said, "You foreign bastard, not you Westy, you've been here for a bit." I didn't know if I was hearing things. In one game, I took a hit and I could see double. I told Howie this and he just advised me, "tackle the inside one."

Paul Woods from Cardiff head-butted me during a game in January 1983. I went into a tackle, he came in with his head and smashed my cheekbone. I kept playing until half time, but realised there was something badly wrong. The doctor took a look at it and said I would have to go to hospital. Off I went to have an x-ray, then they had to push it back out for me. That was hard. I had it done at Rochdale Hospital. I woke up after having the operation sat in a bed on a ward in the middle of the night. I wasn't sure what was going on. They gave me a drink and something to eat, next time I came to it was night time again. At one end of the ward there was a woman moaning, "Ooohhhhhh, ohhhhhhh nurse, there's a fire in the corner." It was explained to me there had been a fire at her house and she was a bit worried. Next thing I heard her shouting, "Here puss puss, here puss puss." I was laughing, there were some characters in those hospitals.

Another time, I went into hospital to get my nose straightened. A few people had told me that they put yards of rope up there after it was broken. They went on to say that it would really hurt when it came out. I came round after my operation and because my nose was blocked, my head felt thick. The nurse told me they would leave it until the morning before taking everything out of my nose. I tried to get them to do it straight away, but to no avail. I managed to get through the night. The fellow in the bed next to me had been moaning all through the night. The doctor pulled the curtains round him and said, "That leg does look bad, you know it might have to come off". I called the nurse over immediately and said, "Don't get our beds mixed up". They took the stuff out of my nose and it didn't hurt at all. The best thing was fresh air coming through my nostrils again, which cleared my head.

We had a game against Fulham in February 1984 and they beat us 22–10 in London. Reggie Bowden was their half-back. He came through and ducked at my challenge; I would have hit him in the chest, but instead cracked him around the head. It dropped him. I said, "Sorry about that Reg, you ducked."

"Oh, don't worry about that, you're going to get yours".

The game went on, but I didn't receive any retribution. When the return fixture took place at Central Park, I found out what he had been talking about. Two of their huge pack belted the hell out of me. Everywhere I went that match, one of them was waiting for me. Reggie was running past, singing, "Told you." I just thought "Well, if you give it, you've got to take it."

We had a season where I thought the training was poor, we would look promising, but things never came off. Half the players lived out of town and we only trained twice a week. We had no momentum.

5. Beating the Australians

At the end of my first season with Wigan I was selected to play for New Zealand against Australia. I played a few club games when I got back there because I wanted to keep fit. We played Inglewood and there was a shower of hailstones. It was still pretty warm though. All the players were saying, "We can't go out and play in this."

"You soft bastards," came my less than sympathetic reply. Having played through a northern winter, this was no big deal to me.

My wife's mum had died just after we had arrived in the UK. She hadn't gone back for the funeral. I told my wife that we would all go back so that she could visit the grave. I asked the selectors if I would be playing and be part of it? They said they would pay for me to come over, but due to the circumstances, I would pay to bring my family over too. They assured me I would be involved. My province had got money out of my transfer so they paid my wife's fare and I paid for the kids. I got there and Graham Lowe, the coach had named me on the bench. I thought: "Ah well, at least I'm a part of it." We ended up getting beat by Australia 16–4 and I only got 10 minutes at the end. I was totally pissed off. I went to them and said, "Fine, I've had a gut's full of it, I'm going back to England once I've played a game for my province."

The provincial game was to be against Wellington which would be a real ding-dong clash. I played for my club side then I got a call from Ron McGregor, the chairman of the New Zealand Rugby League, who told me I had to make myself available for international selection. I told him I was pissed off that after being assured I would be part of the test, I had only got 10 minutes.

I played in the provincial game and Ron McGregor came down. I had an unbelievable game, everywhere I was, the ball turned up. I ended up scoring six tries. We smashed them. After the game, Ron said to me, "You played great, you've got to make yourself available."

"Well I don't have to make myself available, you please yourself."

Mark Graham got injured and they needed someone to take his place. I got another phone call and was asked, "What would you say if you'll play?"

"Fine, I'll play."

I got over to Brisbane and not only was I playing, but Graham Lowe had made me captain. I couldn't understand how I could go from playing for 10 minutes to being captain.

The test was to be played at Lang Park. The training sessions we had on the Monday and Tuesday were a bit lacklustre. Lowe said to me that we needed more out of the training sessions and I said I agreed with him. I went and spoke to the players and said that we were getting ready for a test match against the Australians, had already been beaten by them once and needed to get into it. I felt this was an opportunity to get something really good under our belts and we needed to have a go.

On the Wednesday night, a few of us were walking around Brisbane city centre. Now, one of the things before test matches is that you've got to be occupied. You have a week in camp and you end up in your hotel room looking at the walls. You've got to have something to do. When you're at home, you have your family with you so it's different. In camp, you train, have your shower and that's it. It was American Independence Day and we stumbled across an American bar. It was all go and we thought it looked a bit unusual. "Come on" we said and in we went. We had a couple of beers and a bit of a laugh. We went back to the hotel and everybody was relaxed.

The next two training sessions were bloody marvellous. I don't know why it worked, but it did. We were all really keyed up and maybe that bar helped the players release some tension. We went out and beat Australia on the Saturday 19–12.

Doing the Haka before a game was tremendous. It's funny though that when we beat Australia in 1983 we decided not to do it. We said, "These bastards are used to having the Haka done and they just take the piss out of it". We thought we would do it at the end of the match instead. So we walked out onto the park, just stood there and said, "Let's get on with it". I think it threw the Aussies a little. We kicked off and got into them. We did the Haka after the match and really got stuck into it. That's the only time that's ever happened as far as I know.

At the end of the game we felt drained. We went into the dressing shed and had a drink, the media were there and so on. Once the media had gone and everyone was getting changed, Howie Tamati and I walked out to the side of the Lang Park pitch. There was a sponsors' area with chairs and tables with just a few lights on in the now empty stadium. We just sat there with a can of beer each and said: "Right mate, we've done it."

"Yeah, doesn't it feel good?"

An Aboriginal family came up to us asking for autographs and we ended up having a chat and a laugh with them. We did go out on the town for a few beers afterwards, but it was just a nice moment to take it all in and realise that all the hard work had paid off. We'd started off playing for our clubs, gone through all the steps and ended up beating the world champions in their own backyard. It was another step to where I wanted to get to. To enjoy it with your family is very good.

After the Lang Park game, one of the Australian rugby league writers, Frank Hyde, came into the dressing room and told me I was his man-of-the-match and gave me a watch.

Newspaper coverage of the Kiwis' famous victory over Australia in 1983.

I came back to Britain, went out on the training pitch for Wigan and found out that Murphy had replaced me as captain. It's worth explaining how he made me captain in the first place. During the previous year, I had done a bit of training on my own to try and get things going. On the Saturday, those players who could make it did a bit of extra training. We started winning a few games including beating Leeds and St Helens. We were getting momentum and starting to come together, although Murphy was not involved.

We were playing at Featherstone and Murphy told us we were all going to the races before the match. I looked in disbelief at him and wondered what was going on. We were out in the cheap sections while he was up with the hoi polloi. We got to Featherstone and it was a real close game. We could have won, but right near the end, we got a penalty right near their posts. I wasn't the captain but I was saying, "Shoot for goal, shoot for goal." Murphy was on the sideline screaming, "Tap it! Tap it!"

They looked at Murphy, as the players used to, tapped it and lost the ball on the first tackle. We drew the game 9–9. I came off the pitch ready to have a showdown with Murphy. Bugger me, he'd gone. Bill Ashurst said, "Westy, he's gone with one of the directors back to Wigan. By the way, he's made you captain." I just thought, "What the hell goes on here".

When he took the captaincy off me at the start of the 1983–84 season, he gave it to one of the half-backs, I believe it was Jimmy Fairhurst. After a couple of games, Jimmy got a long term injury so he could no longer skipper the side. It happened during a game so Murphy sent on an assistant with the message, "Who wants to take the captaincy?" I couldn't believe they were going to leave it up to the players. Glyn Shaw, the Welshman stepped up and said he would do it. We got to Hull and Glyn broke his leg, that was him out.

We were out training and I got a message to go and see Maurice Lindsay and Murphy in the office. "Westy, you're going to have to take this captaincy back," said Maurice.

"Why?"

"Well, you're the more experienced one, you're going to have to take it back."

"You want me to take it back?"

"Yes, you will," interjected Murphy now.

44

"Oh so you're asking me? Alright, I will take it back, no problem."

Our relationship was never that good because I'd been through that situation with early test matches. I knew that not having a team structure was detrimental to what people wanted to achieve in a team game. It was necessary to have everybody's strengths and weaknesses ironed out. Everybody had to be playing the same way and singing from the same hymn sheet.

There were a lot of rule changes in the game at this time. I think they made it a better game. The changes that were made had been thought about. The 10 minutes in the sin bin wasn't for things like decapitating somebody. It was used for things like answering the referee back, and other disciplinary issues. I think most of the referees did a good job with it. As a coach, a captain or a teammate if someone was getting out of line you would either sub him or tell him to shut up. Plus if a player got sin binned and the opposition scored the winner in that time, he might not be playing next week.

The sin bin also took the heat out of certain situations. If there was something brewing and a player did something that didn't really warrant a sending off, the referee could utilise the sin bin. It would cool the offender down and he would come back on the pitch a better player for it.

I was given a column in the local newspaper and I criticised the way we were training. I'd had enough and I pointed out that we weren't going to make the strides forward that we could do if we didn't start to train better.

We lost to Warrington 24–6 at Central Park. Maurice Lindsay told me that Murphy wanted to have a word with me in the office and that he wasn't so happy with what I'd put in my column. I told him fine. He warned me again that Murphy wasn't happy and I said, "Whatever." I got to the office and he was very angry with me. He was going mad, he said, "It's you or me at this club." After he'd got it all out of his system, I said, "Look Alex, the only reason I'm here is that I want to do well for me, I want to do well for Wigan because they've signed me, I want to do well for the spectators because there's more of them coming to watch. I don't want to come here as a bum and go through the motions." He repeated, "It's you or me at this club," then he went out and slammed the door.

I opened the door and there was Mary Stretton, one of the women who worked in the office at Wigan. "How did you put up with that?" she asked.

I said: "Listen Mary, I've heard it all before so don't worry so much about it. I've got to put up with it."

The week after we lost to Warrington it was the first round of the Challenge Cup and we were struggling. We had to travel to Bramley. It ended up 10–10 after I scored a try to keep us in the tie. Mark Cannon played centre in that match but was changed to stand-off for the replay at Central Park. He ended up having a great game passing the ball and that's how we started to do better. We won the replay 34–4 and were on the road to Wembley.

We had an easy draw apart from having to beat St Helens at Knowsley Road in the third round. After Bramley we played Oldham at Central Park and then beat York in the semi-final in Leeds.

Wembley was amazing. I used to watch it at home on television. In those days, we only had two channels in New Zealand. I used to watch the Challenge Cup Final and couldn't get over the size of the crowd. In 1983 Kevin and I took our two oldest boys, Damon and Vaughan, who were both aged nine, to the Challenge Cup Final. It was Hull versus Featherstone with all our Kiwi mates playing for Hull. We went down the Hull end and were convinced they were going to win. As the game was kicking off, we looked down and both our boys were asleep under the crash barriers. Kevin and I just looked around thinking how much we would like to play at Wembley. Little did we know the very next year we'd be playing against each other at the same ground. Kevin won in 1984 with Widnes and I went back the following year to win it in 1985 when we beat Hull.

In 1984, for the week of the Wembley final, Alex took us all to Southport. We had a big meal and a few beers, I remember thinking "This shouldn't be." We went down to London really early, on the Tuesday. The players were sailing up and down the Thames eating what they wanted, gambling and having a beer. I didn't think it was the way to go, but Maurice Lindsay said to me, "Alex knows what he's doing, he's been here before."

Our extra training had helped us start winning games and got us to Wembley. Our half-backs, Gary Stephens and Mark Cannon, had been getting the ball out wide which had worked for us. Murphy said to

Stephens, "Gary, you've got to dominate this game." I was trying to tell him to let the ball go like normal. We got to Wembley and Gary tried to do everything himself and got bowled on his arse a couple of times with Joe Lydon scoring at the other end. I just thought that our tactics were wrong. At the end of the game, all the Wigan players were sat around crying. I went round to each of them saying, "What are you doing crying? You didn't play anywhere near well enough to win that game. I never played well enough, as a team we didn't play well enough. We didn't do the things that got us to the final in the first place." Alex could always talk a good game. Mark Cannon got some of the blame following the 1984 final, but in my opinion, Gary Stephens didn't give him the ball. I don't think we'd have won the game anyway, but we would have given a far better account of ourselves if we had played the way we had been doing.

When I got down to Wembley, I could see why people loved the experience so much. It was a whole day out. Some supporters would end up disappointed with the final score, but there was no fighting.

Andy Gregory was a half-back who would always give you a bit of cheek. When I played against him at Wembley in 1984 I went to get him and missed him by very little. The referee, Billy Thompson, called me over and said, "You can get sent off at Wembley as well you know."

"Billy, did I hit him?"

"No, but you can still get sent off at Wembley." Greg was stood behind him yelling, "Give it to him Billy." Somebody gave Greg a picture of that moment with me, with my head down, towering over Billy telling me off while Greg is chirping away just behind him.

After we lost the 1984 final we came back on the coach to Wigan. We had a few beers on the way and were disappointed with the loss. The general consensus was "Have a beer when we got to Wigan and then go home." We got to Central Park and one of the assistants had a look inside the stadium then ran back onto the coach. "You'd better get in there. They're all out there waiting for you."

I asked, "Who?"

"All the speccies, there's about four or five thousand in there waiting for you on the pitch."

I went out on the pitch and couldn't believe it, we were signing autographs for them and so on. I had Dwayne sat on my shoulders and a Wigan hat on my head, I was talking to everybody, it was fantastic. I thought "I'd die to get back to Wembley to repay this support."

Just after that, I got a letter from a local vicar. It said, "Well Graeme, we're really disappointed. We didn't play well. We really thought we'd win, but we all support Wigan."

Now I don't know why I did it but I wrote on the bottom, "Don't worry, we'll get back next year," and posted it back to him.

When we returned triumphant from Wembley the following year, the letter came back to me again with the comment "Paid in full, marvellous." It was signed by the vicar.

Kevin Tamati went to Widnes, then Warrington and Greg followed him to Warrington. We were due to play Warrington and Kevin was telling Greg to get after me. He told him to call me 'Pakeha'. In Maori, that means 'unwanted guest' and is what they called the English when they came to New Zealand. The first scrum goes down and this voice pipes up, "Ey Pakeha". I didn't know who it was coming from but heard it again and realised it was Greg. It's the only time I've ever smacked him. The referee was looking away and the touch judge must have been looking the other way too. I smashed him. "You bully," he shouted as he was jumping up and down about it.

The nickname 'Tex' followed me throughout my career, but I'm buggered if I know where it came from. I think it may have originated from Mark Graham when I roomed with him in Great Britain, maybe something to do with me being long and tall. It must have got around because Andy Gregory still calls me that to this day.

Being part of that team early on, some of the players were at different levels, but they were all giving it their best shot. Some of them got better, some of them fell away as we all do eventually. It was good to be a part of something that was growing. We started off with crowds of 3,500 and they started creeping forward and kept creeping forward. We eventually got up to 15,000 to 16,000 on average and it was fantastic to be a part of it. I played the game to play in front of big crowds like that.

Shaun Edwards was breaking into the team at this stage and one thing we knew about Shaun was that he had a heart as big as a lion. When he first came through, Murphy played him at stand-off. He was a great young player, but he kept taking people on. Some of the older, more experienced opposition players were giving him a bit of a hiding.

48

He'd get cut, we'd go to the next scrum and Shaun would take them on again. Being inexperienced at that stage, he must have thought he could do what he had done at schoolboy level. He was only a kid himself though and was playing against experienced men that knew what they were doing. I knew if he learnt and gained some experience, he was going to be one hell of a player. He went to centre and then full-back. We could see at full-back where he had more room to move that he was a player with a lot of talent. It was inevitable that he would go back to the halves because that's what he was signed as. He was learning his craft. He came back to the halves and he was magnificent. If I was picking my team and wanted a dominant half-back who could play a magnificent team game, I'd pick Shaun.

Another player from this period at Wigan was John Pendlebury. He was a great player and really committed to the game. He wasn't big, but was strong and worked hard. He used to play a real loose-forward's game by laying the ball off and running the angles. He used to make me laugh. At one stage, they had him working on the ground staff at Central Park. He was very opinionated and if you got into an argument with him, he wouldn't back down, especially when it got to politics. He left Wigan during the 1984–85 season to join Salford.

In the end, Murphy got pushed down the road in quite an amazing set of circumstances. At the beginning of the 1984–85 season we had the Wigan Sevens. I wasn't selected for the seven-a-side that year. I believe Colin Clarke and Alan McInnes were coaching the side. They had done really well in Murphy's absence throughout the tournament. Just before the final, Murphy came in from the airport back from his holiday. He strode across the pitch, chest puffed out. Anyway, Wigan won the final. By the sound of it, he went into the office the next morning to get his pay packet, but there was no pay there because he hadn't done the job. The other coaches had done the job right through. There was an argument. I came in the next morning and one of the men on the car park told me, "Murphy's been sacked". I thought he was kidding. I went into the office and Maurice was still very shaken. "I've sacked him," he said.

"Thank Christ for that," I thought, "There is a God after all." I started smiling. That particular night, we were due for training, Colin Clarke and Alan McInnes took us for the session. It was one of the hardest training sessions I've ever done, but everybody at the end of it was still smiling. It was such a load off everybody's mind. They came in and did the things we should have been doing in the first place. They put a structure in place and away we went. We did well in the league, won the Challenge Cup and got to the final of the Lancashire Cup, just losing to Saints. We also got to the semi-final of the Premiership. It was quite a good year.

That was the start of everything. At one stage earlier, after Murphy had had his go at me, the club must have thought I was teetering on the brink of heading somewhere else. After a game, I was in the player's bar and the directors had come down to see me, they told me, "Stick with it, we know what's going on, stick with it."

I was always looking at my own performance, trying to get better, fitter and stronger. At one stage, I went through a spell of trying to get up quickly and play the ball to myself if there was no-one in front of me to get some quick yards. I kept cocking it up and had to remember "Don't bloody do it".

There were times that I got dropped. When Colin and Alan first took over, they took me to the coaches' room, told me they didn't think I was playing well enough and they were dropping me to the bench. I told them I didn't go along with that, but fine. It helped me take a look at my own game. I trained extra hard and the week after I was back in the side. I understood it and used it later when I was a coach. If there was a player who wasn't performing as well as I thought they could, I gave them a little reminder. I did it once with Shaun Edwards and when he accepted it, I was amazed at the way he came back, he was absolutely flying.

The 1984 Challenge Cup Final

Graeme, Brian Juliff and Brian Case celebrate reaching Wembley in 1984 after beating York in the Challenge Cup semi-final.

Leading the team out at Wembley in the 1984 Challenge Cup Final.
(Courtesy *Wigan Observer*)

Tackled by Mike O'Neill in the 1984 Challenge Cup Final.
(Courtesy *Wigan Observer*)

6. Winning the Challenge Cup

The 1984–85 Lancashire Cup Final was between Wigan and Saints at Central Park. We didn't play well in the first half. We were under the cosh and weren't making good field position. As a result, the backs couldn't operate properly. At half time, we came in and took stock. We went out and got back at them in the second half. If it had gone on another 10 minutes, we might have had them. It wasn't to be, they played magnificently and it was a great game.

It was very much like the Challenge Cup Final later that season when we beat Hull. That day, we played great in the first half, but they could have got us right at the whistle. That's what makes exciting games. I've had Saints fans in my taxi reminding me of that Lancashire Cup Final and also the Premiership semi-final later in the season on the Wednesday after Wembley which Saints also won. They then say that was the year Mal Meninga was here playing for Saints. I just tell them they beat us fair and square in both games. There were a lot of good players on show at that time. Hull had Kemble, Leuluai, Ah Kuoi, O'Hara and Sterling. St Helens had Mal! Great player. We had Brett Kenny and John Ferguson. People back then, as they do now, wanted to see stars from overseas, but they also wanted to see young English players coming through too.

Over a period of time, young English players came through at Wigan and became world class performers. That's why if the clubs got the system right in the game today, they wouldn't need to rely on so many imports from overseas. They could still bring in top stars, but they wouldn't need to sign ordinary players to fill holes in the team.

We played Hull KR in the Challenge Cup semi-final. During the game, I passed to David Stephenson for a key try. It was actually a set move. Colin and Alan had been talking about how we could tap the ball in the middle on the 20 metre line and take it up, making about three or four yards at the most. Their view was everyone was so set on taking up the middle because they didn't want to make a mistake and that we should try something different. We put two passes out wide from the tap, I came onto it and there was a hole in the defence. We had practiced it in training and it worked like a dream. I saw Hull KR full-back George Fairbairn coming up so took him one way then went round the other side and unloaded to Stephenson. One minute George was there, the next he was behind me.

For the last try I went down the blind side, drew the cover in, and popped it over the top for Gilly to score. We won 18–11. The best thing about the game was that the forwards were making the breaks. At Wigan that year, our two wingers were in the top 10 try scorers. Kenny and Edwards both bagged quite a few too.

In the final itself, we went out to play how we had done throughout the year. We had learnt our lesson from the previous year. The coaching staff were great, the players were all set up for it and everything was right. The week of the game, Brett Kenny had an idea to get the team fund going. It was something called "beetles and penguins". He explained that if somebody yelled out "penguins" we'd have to get in a line behind each other and waddle like penguins. The last one to do it had to chuck a fiver into the team fund. It was the same idea with the shout of "beetles" except that we had to get on our backs waving our arms and legs in the air. So, the week of the final, this was going on and it included all the directors who had come down with us and all the coaching staff. It had to be done at the right time and not at anything formal although one or two did try. The big laugh was the directors. We were based at Wasps rugby union ground in London for training during the week and somebody shouted "penguins". One sprinted across so he didn't have to pay the fiver. Another one just sat there with his cigar saying, "I'll pay".

There was another time we were on our way back from a game and all the directors fell asleep on the coach. One of the players pulled out a pair of scissors and snipped Tom Rathbone's tie halfway up. Tom finally stirred as we turned the corner into Central Park and said to Jack Robinson, "Look, what they've done to my tie." I ended up feeling so sorry for the old boy I let him have my tie.

It was a red hot day when we played Hull at Wembley. Despite that, we only ended up using one of our subs. When a team has a decent lead and the other side start to come back, the coach has to weigh up whether it's right to make a change or not. In the first half, everything was going great. Then in the second half we made a couple of mistakes and they started coming back at us. We were trying to shore things up and fill in the gaps. Players like Peter Sterling knew how to find gaps though. If they had done that in the first half, we'd have probably been on the end of a bit of a towelling. Fortunately, we had players who could do the same. It was an evenly matched final. We just managed to make more of our opportunities.

Going up for the cup as captain was fantastic; it was the culmination of an incredible couple of hours. We started off the afternoon by walking up the tunnel, there was a bit of a slope up to the top and we could hear some noise. As we got up to the top of the tunnel, the noise hit us like a wall of sound. The old Wembley, at that time, was all standing behind the goals so all we would see was a sea of heads, hats, flags and scarves. There could be 15 fans to a square yard whereas if it was seated there might be two. It was unbelievable. We wanted to try and take it in, but we also wanted to concentrate on the game and what we needed to do. Then we would meet the dignitaries and as captain I would introduce them to my team mates and so on. It's at the end of the game when we could relax and think "Thank Christ for that". Then we could go and enjoy ourselves.

Mike Ford was a great little scrum-half. I thought in the 1984–85 season he was one of the links and kingpins of the side. Brett Kenny did some marvellous things from stand-off, but Fordy did very well at scrum-half. In the lead up to the 1985 Wembley final I did some promotional work on television for a programme called *Focus*. After the game, they had a portable television set to give away to the player I felt had been man-of-the-match. Shaun Edwards had played really well at full-back, but I felt Fordy had done a great job in providing the link between the forwards and Kenny. I gave my man of the match to Fordy as Kenny had already got the Lance Todd Trophy.

It was a good night after the final although to be fair, it had been the year before too. I remember Billy Boston would always come to London with us, a great fellow Billy. Whenever we won a trophy, we would always take it over to his pub The Griffin, which was just by Central Park, before Maurice Lindsay could take it elsewhere. The pub would be splitting at the sides with people standing on pool tables and having a great time.

Anyway, after the loss to Widnes in 1984, Billy said, "It didn't go so well boys, but never mind, I'll get the first round in." Henderson Gill asked for a pint of milk, I had half a lager and Billy had a pint. It came to £17. You should have seen the look on Billy's face. When we lost, it was still important to enjoy the night. But it was not the same feeling.

55

The 1985 Challenge Cup Final

Leading the team out at Wembley in 1985.

With the Cup after our dramatic win over Hull (Courtesy *Rugby League Journal*)

Top: Lifting the Challenge Cup at Wembley in 1985. (Courtesy *Wigan Observer*)

Left: Celebrating with John Ferguson after the final hooter at Wembley.

Arriving back at Central Park in 1985 to a rapturous welcome.

Thanking the fans for their support at Wembley.

Players just think it's time for a holiday and then start again for the next season. After winning in 1985 it was a different feeling, it was the epitome of being a rugby league player, we'd actually done it. Coming through Wigan in 1985 on the open top bus after the final was an amazing experience too.

One of the directors who I really liked was old Jack Hilton. After a game where we had put in everything we had but still lost, Jack would come into the dressing room and say, "Listen fellows, you put in a real good effort today. If you put that effort in next week you'll win." We'd say, "Thanks Jack." That's the difference between a person who's played the game and one who hasn't. Jack had been a great player in his time and knew what he was talking about when it came to talking to players. He got my respect. The other directors got their respect in the way they handled the club.

The wingers in the 1984–85 team were Henderson Gill and John Ferguson. They were both fantastic players, but with contrasting personalities. Henderson was bubbly and always jumping around, John was quiet and unassuming, but they both worked well in the team. Gilly scored some fantastic long range tries. With John, a player could make a break and be tackled, he would get to half back and get through the gap before the defence could close it down; it was fantastic to watch.

That year was a great year; the team played some wonderful open rugby. Our two wingers were in the top ten try scorers. In some of the games the backs would be a bit muted so the forwards would do the job. In most of the games though, the backs would do the job. We had Brett Kenny, Mike Ford, Steve Donlan, David Stephenson, John Ferguson, Henderson Gill and Shaun Edwards. It was a really good side and the players complemented each other. The pack was there to lay the platform for the backs to play off. Neil Courtney was big for a prop, but gee he knew what he was doing. He was experienced and knew how to play the game. Then Brian Case, Brian Dunn and Ian Potter. There was also Nicky Kiss at hooker, what a character he was.

While there were a lot of New Zealanders in England, we would have a do on Christmas Day at Wigan St Judes Rugby League Club. We had a big dinner together. We could not have a drink before Boxing Day, but we could go out that night. It was the same with New Year's Day after that game. Not only were the players out, but the fans were as well so it was always a good night. The pubs did really well out of it.

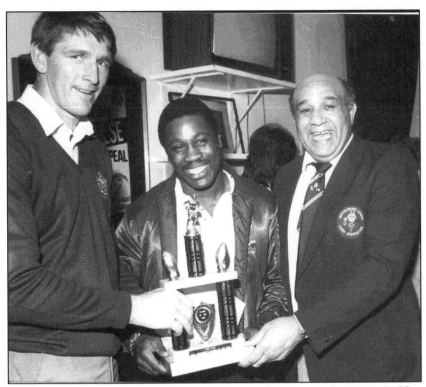
With Henderson Gill and Billy Boston when Henderson won the Wigan RLFC Vice-Presidents' Player-of-the-Year award in 1985 (Courtesy *Wigan Observer*)

After five years, the overseas quota came down to three players per club. Kevin Tamati and I thought that our clubs wouldn't want us because we were getting a bit long in the tooth. We felt clubs would be looking for young, up-and-coming players. So, we decided to do a big trip around Europe with both our families. We did 8,000 miles by car in two months. It was a marvellous time and we went everywhere. We went down as far as Dubrovnik in Yugoslavia. We were camping through Eurocamp and where they didn't have tents, we used our own. When we got back, we found out that David Oxley, through the Rugby Football League, had made us exempt from the quota because we had given five years good service. As a result, we could stay. I've got to thank them for that. We loved the tour out of sight, but the only reason we had done it was because we thought we would be going home. I'm glad it happened.

The next season, 1985–86, we had another good campaign and won the John Player Special Trophy. At the end of the season, the club then decided they wanted to change to a full-time coaching staff. Graham Lowe came over from Australia as a result. Colin and Alan were going to take the club to a tribunal over their dismissal. I then did something I will always regret. Like a dumb bastard, I behaved the way I had believed in New Zealand where everything goes to the club. All your efforts go to the club and nobody gets anything out of the club. One of the directors asked me if I would go to the tribunal and speak against Colin and Alan. I said I would and that's what I did. I always regretted that. As I've gone on through life in the game, I know what goes on at clubs. I have learnt different aspects of how things are handled. I always look back and think I did them a wrong one. It's one of the rare things I look back on that was negative and I could have done without. For how they had taken the club forward and what they had done for the club, they deserved better than that. Life's not always about making the right decisions, sometimes people make the wrong decisions, you've just got to be able to make the right ones next time.

We beat Hull KR 11–8 at Elland Road in the John Player Special Trophy final. That was the year Wigan brought over Greg Dowling and Steve Ella. Steve had been brought over to replace Brett Kenny. They had both played in the same Parramatta side. Steve was a good player and distributed the ball like Kenny had. He was a really hard worker. Dowling had been brought over after Neil Courtney had got injured. I really liked Neil, he was an old fashioned forward. He could certainly play though and did really well.

During the off season though, we were training at Robin Park. Neil slipped and severed an artery in his shoulder. There was a big sack of blood hanging from his shoulder. He had to go to hospital. His nerve there is now like mine is today and he has lost full use of his arm. He couldn't use his hand and his arm was semi paralysed. Sadly, he had to give up the game as a result. Dowling was different, a good player, but I thought very full of himself. Some of the English players thought him a bit arrogant. He did his job though.

There were some players who were very serious in the dressing room then there were players such as Joe Lydon, who we had signed from Widnes, who would be telling jokes. John Ferguson used to lie on the benches and just relax. There were some players who would have to have their right underpants. I was amazed when I first came over that the kit man used to provide everything from swimming trunk type undies to tie ups for our socks. Players would be shouting where a particular pair of undies was and Taffy would shout back, "They're in the bloody wash." Then there were players who would want to go out second. On the other hand some players wanted to go out last. There would be two of them taking ages tying their boots wanting to go out last and I'd yell, "Fucking get out there." I'd have to kick them up the arse to get them out the door.

Shaun Wane was a character and would have some fun in the changing rooms; he was always full of himself. He was shadow boxing one day and I warned him, "Look out for the left". I hit him and he told me his mouth was bleeding, I apologised, but reminded him I had told him to look for the left. Another time he came out of the shower and tried wrestling with me, I got him on his back to hear the excuse, "I've got no clothes on." He was a great character, had a heart as big as a lion and in the pack I'd have him beside me any day.

In August 1985 we went over to the Isle of Man to play in the Charity Shield. I had never been there so it was a new place to go. We jumped on the ferry to go over and the crossing was very rough. We decided to go for a meal in the restaurant. The ship was bouncing up and down. Martin Dermott's face appeared at a port hole, he was green. He ended up spewing over the side of the boat. When we got there, the most striking thing was coming around a corner and seeing Douglas. It looked like we had gone back to the 1940s, it reminded me of Patrick McGoohan's place in *The Prisoner*. It was a great place though, very friendly and both sets of supporters enjoyed themselves. We beat Hull KR 34–6 and there was a good celebration afterwards. We went over there again to play Halifax.

We won three trophies that season and it was the start of the big Wigan run of success. It was a combination of things. Graham Lowe had arrived and things went up another notch with him being a full-time coach. He had more experience with having coached in Australia. A lot more players started coming into the club, great players and the club started doing very well.

The first team had a better work ethic together at this time. One thing Graham Lowe was good at was talking the game up. He would come in with a move like the flying wedge where close to the line one person would take the ball in with everyone else behind him pushing like a scrum. They were unusual moves, but seemed to work. He was a Winston Churchill type too, he used to make speeches and bang the desk. He got a bit emotional and had health problems. The only trophy we didn't win in 1986–87 was the Challenge Cup after we got knocked out at Oldham. It was pissing it down that day and was a close game. We had a kick to touch that didn't go out. They brought the ball back and Paddy Kirwan managed to sneak through and score. It was so late in the game that many supporters had left for home thinking Wigan had won. Every dinner I went to after that game Paddy would be introduced as "the man who had beaten Wigan."

Wigan picked up their first league title in 27 years in 1986–87. Ellery Hanley and Joe Lydon had come in during the previous season. Ellery was an exceptional player. Not only could he score tries, but he could read the game, he could see where the ball was and he would be there to make the try. He would be on hand to finish things off. Shaun Edwards learnt a lot from him in that respect. Shaun clicked on pretty quickly that Ellery would be right on the inside or outside of someone making a break. He was good at it anyway, but he got better.

Ellery was a great player and around that era, he was probably one of the best players that there was. He was an individual. He went out and gave his best on the park, which always showed. He was an unusual character, he would finish the game and then away he went. That was his choice I suppose. Everybody else stuck around. There were players I would have a beer with, then there were players I would play alongside who I knew very well but I didn't have a beer with. Then there would be others I wouldn't be bothered about having a beer with. I still played alongside them and did the job.

Andy Goodway was focussed and wanted to do well in games which is good. He concentrated on what he needed to do to succeed. Andy Platt was very quiet. He was a bit dry sometimes with some of his sayings. When I first started playing against him, he was playing second-row at St Helens. He came to Wigan later on.

Steve Hampson – or 'Hampo' as he was known – was a bloody tormentor. We'd go to parties and he'd been giving everyone a hard time. He was the organiser of what would be going on during the week. He was really unlucky because he broke his leg before finals a couple of times. He was a fantastic catcher of the ball; I'd never seen anyone catch a ball like him with the possible exception of Greg Brentnall, the Australian full-back. Hampo did a lot of trampoline work which assisted him. Even today, he's tremendously fit. He was tremendously focussed on the game, wanted to do well and if he thought something was wrong, he'd tell people about it.

We played Warrington at Bolton in the 1986–87 John Player Special Trophy final. Martin Dermott was selected for the game at hooker. We had played them at Wigan on New Year's Day and they had beaten us by two points. It had been a real ding-dong tussle that day. I knew the final would be more of the same 10 days later. I was up playing number 8 and just thought "Whatever happens, happens." Dermott was still quite young at this point. I remember thinking that Les Boyd would have a go at him. He did give him a couple of tackles but by and large he left him alone. He beat the crap out of our Australian forward Ian Roberts though. Robert's chin ended up split open and I thought "That's great from your Aussie team mate." They had a ferocious pack including Boyd and Kevin Tamati. That's why I didn't think picking 'Derm' was sensible, but his form had been good. In the end, it turned out to be a great selection because he played well and we won 18–4.

The standout memory for me from that game involved Les Boyd. Boydy hated Henderson Gill. Gilly was a cheeky player and was saying all sorts to him. Boydy was snorting, trying to get hold of him. We were attacking their line and were about 20 metres out. Gilly took the ball and ran across the line, Boydy shot out to smack him, and Gilly stepped inside him and scored under the posts. I've never seen Les Boyd so distraught in all my life. He was stamping his feet and going wild. I laughed all the way back to the halfway line. Boydy, like the rest of that Warrington pack, had a reputation. We beat them though, so that reputation went out the window.

I played with Kurt Sorenson at test level and he was a hell of a competitor. He put me on my arse in one game when we played Widnes in the Premiership. I was just about to pass the ball and he hit me a bloody pearler. I banged the back of my head on the ground, got up and had the wobbly gumboot on. I was trying to walk straight, but it just didn't work. He was a great, strong player.

I was captain until the 1987–88 season. I had a word with Maurice and said that Ellery Hanley and Shaun Edwards were becoming more experienced, were very capable players and it would be better if one of them took the captaincy. Lowe had sort of settled on his team and there were only two subs back then. I was being put on the bench at times, sometimes with Ray Mordt. I thought, "What's the use of training and ending up on the bench, I want to play." I went to Lowe and said, "Look, you please yourself but I want to be playing. I want to go into the 'A' team." He warned me that I might not get selected for first team as a result. I told him I wasn't bothered. I went back and played for the 'A' team for a few weeks.

He had put me on the bench for the World Club Challenge game against Manly, but once we started winning, he wouldn't put me on. He wanted to do it with all English players. Dean Bell was injured at the time so I was the only overseas player in the squad that game. I wasn't particularly disappointed, but often wondered if Wigan had been losing, would Lowe have used me. That was his choice and I got paid winning pay for sitting on my arse.

Then Lowe had a big bust up with Hanley. Lowe wanted Hanley to rest while Hanley wanted to play and words were exchanged. Hanley did not play for about six weeks. Lowe came to me and said he wanted me to play second-row in the first team in the Challenge Cup. I said that was no problem. Away we went, we beat all the top teams on the way through to Wembley to face Halifax in 1988. However, Lowe made up with Ellery and I got dropped.

One of the good things about the situation was that in 1985 I had taken Shaun Wane out of Wembley. It had been during the semi-final against Hull KR, I had gone into make a tackle, swung round and taken Shaun's knee out. He had scored a try in that game and was playing really well; I had buggered him for the final. Shaun got the subs spot for the 1988 final though. That was a good thing about me missing out.

I was disappointed to miss that 1988 Wembley final because it would have been my last big game for the club, but I was pleased that Shaun Wane finally got his chance on the big day.

My brother had come over from New Zealand to see the final and I wasn't playing so I was a bit fed up. That's the way it goes.

On the attack for Wigan (Courtesy *Wigan Observer*)

Celebrating winning the John Player Special Trophy.

7. Player-coaching the 'A' team

Around 1988 the club asked if I would consider player-coaching the 'A' team, it sounded a good idea to me and a natural progression. From 1985 onwards I had also been working on fundraising for the club, a scheme known as the Knights of Central Park. I worked as pools officer so with being 'A' team coach as well I was at the club all the time. In the pools office my boss was Billy Blan. He was a past great player for the club, who died in 2008 aged 86. I would run things by him. He was a great fellow to bounce things off and gave me really good information and advice. We had some great chats.

Some very good players came into the 'A' team, such as Ian Lucas, Denis Betts, Phil Clarke, Timmy Street and Richard Russell. We would win everything, then they'd be taken up to the first team and we'd have to start again.

For some periods I had part of a team and when they all got good enough, they'd go through to the first team. Some of them would drop back, such as Ian Potter and Brian Case and have to be sold because they were too experienced to play 'A' team rugby. I'd have no experienced players left so I'd have to build it up again. There were times where I would go to St Pats and St Judes to get second and third team players to fill spots in the 'A' team. I even had to use some of Billy Boston's pub team in the 'A' team on occasion. We got some of our better wins during those times.

Wigan used to play us motivational tapes, there would be 'big hits' tapes, tapes of us scoring tries then there would be American Football tapes where a team were making lots of mistakes, they were struggling, but then they started to work at it and began to fly. As player-coach I couldn't do too much; however, every now and again I had to do something different. I would search my mind to come up with something different for a particular game. Some things worked, some things didn't.

Lowe always wanted to be the first to do things; to be honest, I didn't like him much. As a coach, he had a good record, but I thought he was a bit funny with me. It went back to 1983 in New Zealand when he only used me for 10 minutes at the end of the first test after I had flown over from England and had been told I would definitely play. As I said earlier, I then said I did not want to be considered for selection under those terms. When I was brought back for the second test, he had made me captain. Did he want to embarrass me by making me captain because he thought we might lose again? After we won, maybe there was always going to be something between him and me in the future; he may have thought "I'll show this bloke".

With the way some decisions were made, Lowe went down in my estimation. I don't have any love for him. I look at people like that and thank them for showing me those things because I didn't want to do the same to anyone in the future. I would rather speak to players, explain why they are not being picked and try and help them regain form. I like to try and inform people and that's what it taught me. A coach needs to be able to communicate with people and I've kept that with me all throughout my career. It's like when players find out they've been dropped from a side in the papers. That's wrong. A coach should always tell the team first then announce the side to the press.

Graham Lowe left the club in June 1989 and was replaced by John Monie. He was really good to work with. The first team were winning trophies but ended up with a big backlog of games. There were occasions where I would be needed to go and fill a gap and would go and play for the first team. I had a good relationship with John. He used to come to all the 'A' team games and there was good banter between us. He talked to me about players like Andy Farrell and Mick Cassidy. He would say that he would give them 10 minutes action in the first team to gain experience, but they would come back and play for me. Then there would be times where the 'A' team would be in a cup final and I would be given certain players to play. It was good and I really enjoyed working with him. He was very successful.

Monie was great with me though because he'd work with me. As the 'A' team we won the Alliance Challenge Cup twice, the league title three times and the Lancashire Shield once. The main idea of it though was to make our kids good enough to go through to the first team. Most of those that weren't good enough for our first team were good enough to be sold to other clubs. There were very few that went by the wayside.

Frano Botica or Bots as he was known came over from New Zealand, I think he had been bought by the directors and John Monie wasn't too sure about him. He played on the wing initially and then picked up a knee injury. The 'A' team got through to the Lancashire

Shield final and we were umming and aahing over who we would put in at stand-off. Botica was fit by this stage and John Monie said I could play him if I wanted to. I gave him a shot at stand-off and he had a great game. I think he played one more game for me in the 'A' team then went through to the first team and claimed the stand-off spot.

I had Denis Betts in the 'A' team and he was a real good pro. Denis and Clarkey were in the back-row in the 'A' team for me. I made Clarkey captain. Bettsy was a real fitness fanatic and wanted to do well. I could see that nothing was going to stop him. The things he didn't have in his game he would make up for with his other qualities. He worked on his weaknesses, but any weaknesses he did have in his game were more than compensated by the things that he did well.

We went to Huddersfield once. Now I had heard about this massive Huddersfield team of the 1940s and 1950s. Now they were languishing at the bottom of the league. We walked into the place and it was like walking back into the 1940s. It was an old wooden stadium with a big, ornate scoreboard. It must have housed 30,000 people in its heyday. It was eerie actually, they had wire netting about a third of the way up the stand because the supporters couldn't go any further up into it because it was a fire hazard. I wasn't playing in this particular game, I had selected a team that I felt could go out there and do the job. The game got going and Bettsy had a run in with one of their players. I looked at him and thought I had better get him off. Just before I could do so, a scrum went down. Suddenly, it broke up, Bettsy hit this fellow a few times, I watched him slowly sink to the ground. That was it, he was sent off before I could get him off. I think because Bettsy had already played a few first team games by this point, there was a bit of animosity, a sort of "I'll show you Mr big time". But after that he had a good disciplinary record.

Phil Clarke was always a serious player. When he was playing, everything had to be really right for him to play. When he was in that frame of mind, he played exceptionally well. I saw his serious approach to the game, how he handled players and I thought he would make a good captain. I made him captain of the 'A' team and he did a good job. We won a few trophies with him as captain. He would have a laugh, but would be thinking about what he should and shouldn't do in a game. He didn't like anything ruffling his feathers, he had to be right to play.

Success with the 'A' team. (Courtesy: *Wigan Observer*)

Winning the Cup with the 'A' team
(David Williams, *rlphotos.com*)

Mike Forshaw was a young Wiganer and a character. He and Ian Gildart were good mates. They would always be in the gym training together. Mick Cassidy and Andrew Farrell were the same later on. I thought Forshaw was a bit vain, always looking in the mirror and doing his hair. He played well; he was just a bit unlucky that we had a back-row at the time of Betts, Clarke and Faz. Gildart and Forshaw ended up having to move away from Wigan to get a first team place somewhere else.

Andrew Farrell used to be in the gym all the time and everyone could see he was intent on doing well. I made Faz captain of the 'A' team and later the first team. He would go out, was able to command the team and have the ability to display his talent. He worked for the team and when it came for his time to shine, he was able to do what he needed to do plus more. He was driving everybody to do that little bit extra. I was very lucky to have those players. I had Clarkey then Faz. But there were also good players around them.

A case in point is a player many people might not have heard off, he was called Brendan Barr. He was a young player and he played number ten. I was playing number eight in the 'A' team with him at the time and we used to compete. He never really hit the standard he needed to get to make the first team, but he worked his socks off. He had a job during the day and we would be ready to leave for the 'A' team games about four o'clock for an evening match. He would get dropped off about a mile away at ten to four, then he'd run in his work clothes carrying his gear to the coach. That's the way he was.

During a game, he'd just run and run. He was quite a big fellow, but I've never seen a player motor like him. We would do 400 metre circuits and Brendan would be up with Kris Radlinski. I remember Kris looking over his shoulder, thinking "How has he got here?" Brendan helped a lot of those players come through. He worked tremendously hard during the game. For me, he was like an icon. He might have been one that didn't make it to the first team, but he helped so many others make it. He had a heart as big as a lion. As a fellow, you could see he was happy with life. He just loved playing the game. After moving away from Wigan to play, he came back and played for St Judes. When he left Wigan I said to one of the directors, "Look, this fellow is giving so much of his time and effort to helping these kids come through, let him go for nothing".

"No, we've got to get money, we can get a grand for him," replied the director.

"Ok, why don't you get it and give it to him?"

He said no though, I thought it was bit mean myself considering the amount of money they had paid other players and the small amount Brendan had been on.

I got on really well with David Myers, he was really affable. I would always have a great time with him, although I thought he was daft in some ways. He would sometimes do the stuff that young fellows do. David was playing really well in the first team when the club bought Martin Offiah, even so, he had no qualms about coming back to play for me in the 'A' team. That was the type of man he was. Tragically, he got killed in a car crash and I went to his funeral. There were an awful lot of people at his funeral so he must have been well thought of around the Widnes area. I could understand why, he was a really likeable character. He always had a smile on his face and was always up for a bit of a laugh.

He and Bobbie Goulding were good mates, Bobbie was a character. I got on really well with him though he'd have his say, but he too was a good young man. In the 'A' team there could be someone who was being a bit unruly and I'd have to kick their arse. When Bobbie first came to the club he was playing for his old man's team in Widnes. I told him, "You're mine now, no more games for your dad."

"Oh, but they've got a big game coming up," replied Bobbie.

"No more games for your dad, you're being paid by us, you're here".

Anyway, he came back in a few days later with his tail between his legs, I'd heard through the grapevine he'd been sent off playing for his dad's team and had got a suspension.

"What did I tell you?" I asked.

He started to try and give his reasons but I cut him off, "No buts, you're here. Right, you don't play this week."

He came back the next week, bouncing into the dressing room ready to play. I knew it was a game we would win anyway so told him, "This is my situation, if you want to go and play for your dad, fuck off and play for your dad. You're not playing for me this week, go and play for your dad, take a game's suspension from me".

He complained bitterly about it. His dad came into see me to complain too and I explained, "If he wants to go a play for you let him go and play for you." He didn't play for his dad anymore after that. In the 'A' team there were characters, good kids and good players. There were just some things they had to learn on the way through.

I played alongside Tony Iro in the 'A' team. He came and played wing in the 'A' team. He killed them, we had the likes of Augustine (Gus) O'Donnell at hooker and Bobbie at half-back. We also had Steve Blakeley too so even in the 'A' team we had players who could move the ball about. Tony made the most of it as he was big and strong. He didn't stay long in the 'A' team. He had only come over to Wigan as Kevin's brother, but he ended up playing for the first team regularly.

Mick Cassidy was another who played for me. When he first came to the club, he was very small. I was player-coaching the 'A' team and we went to play at Castleford which was always a tough place to play, even at 'A' team level. I had spoken to John Monie before the game and we had decided that whether we were winning or losing, we would put Cassidy on with quarter of an hour to go and give him a shot. We were losing, Cassidy came on and got knocked out. I remember saying to Jack Robinson, "I don't know if he's going to do any good." Cassidy made me eat my words. He picked up and became an evergreen. He just kept playing and playing to a really high standard. Whatever you wanted him to do, he would do. He was a sociable young guy too and a part of the camaraderie that went on.

During the time Clarkey was in the 'A' team, we had an end of season 'A' team trip to the Isle of Man. As we got on the coach getting ready to set off, the lads brought out all these t-shirts. My second name is Leonard and the t-shirt's read 'Leonard's Lions trip to the Isle of Man'. They were all laughing, shouting, "We know your second name." We got there and one of the lads, who played a bit for the first team, was known for being blessed in the trouser department. I was walking down the promenade and there he was going down the road like a kangaroo with no clothes on. It was dragging along the ground. I ran down to have a word with him. Just as I got to him, the police pulled up alongside and said, "If he doesn't get his clothes on he's booked." I told them not to worry as I bollocked the player.

Another time, Shaun Edwards came away with us. The players had made the rule that every time someone came down to the bar, they had to drink a pint in one in front of everybody. Shaun sneaked out of the front door and went for a run. The players all went mad at this as they saw his head bobbing past the window. The pub we stayed at was across the road from the beach. The players started a call 'hit the beach'. When the call was made, they all had to strip off down to their underpants and head off to the beach, jump in the water and come back. I was hedging back a bit, trying to sneak round a corner to be told, "You too". Away I went. There were little old ladies out for their evening stroll. I was just coming back up when one of the players yanked off my undies and sprinted away with them. That type of camaraderie was a big part of life with the 'A' team.

I used to hold an extra training session sometimes. Now Brendan Barr would work hard all week in his job and at training; we usually played on a Saturday so he liked his Saturday night drinks. I called a training session on a Sunday morning at our training ground at the back of the stand at Central Park. It had snowed. Brendan came in, his eyeballs all over the place, clearly struggling from the night before. We had a great training session and Brendan killed them. He felt as rough as a bear's arse but he was into it. He hit the tackle bags, he hit everything above grass, there was snow flying everywhere. In fact, the session ended with a snowball fight.

When Barrie-Jon Mather first came to the club, I was working in the pools office. His granddad brought him into the club. His granddad had been a Wigan bobby of yesteryear and had a fearsome reputation particularly among visiting supporters to Central Park. Barrie-Jon came in with his brother and I saw that he was big, tall and rangy. His granddad just said, "This is the fellow you want for your team." I thought that he looked the size so I suggested we give him a go. We put him in the 'A' team second-row and he played really well. They moved him to centre and away he went. The problem later on was that negotiations over his contract with the club didn't go so well. He joined Perth Western Reds to link up with John Dorahy, then Castleford and later went to rugby union. He played for Great Britain at rugby league and England at union so he definitely had talent.

While I was coaching the 'A' team I found out that Bradford were interested in me going there. I went to Maurice to have a chat with him about it and he said, "I don't think Bradford would be a place for you to go, they like their own people, they stick to their fellow Yorkshiremen."

I told him I probably went along with that and stayed at the club. I was enjoying myself at Wigan anyway so it would have taken a lot for me to have gone somewhere else.

In 1990–91 I came out of the 'A' team to play late on in the season against Castleford for the first team. John Monie was very intense, but I liked him. Wigan were up for a lot of trophies but because of that, the games mounted up at the end of the year and he was short of bodies. He asked me if I would play at number 10.

"Yeah, I'll play anywhere man."

I went on, did my stint then came off to have a rest. They brought me back on again and I spied the ball on the right hand side. I saw Ellery getting ready in his usual place to get the ball. I saw Greg with the ball and I was stood just inside Ellery and I thought "I'm having this." I went through on the inside, took the ball and scored by the posts. I think it was the first time anyone had ever beaten Ellery for the ball. I timed it just right and it brought the house down.

I even played another game after that against Featherstone in the Premiership. I always loved playing for the club and I was there to play if needed. At the same time, if I wasn't getting the games that I needed I would step back and play in the 'A' team; that was no problem. Some players wouldn't do that.

Nobody could be the big star at Wigan, there were times where Ellery was a great player, Shaun Edwards, the list goes on and on. The club had great players coming out of its ears. Ellery was a great player but he couldn't win a game stood on the pitch on his own. It's a team thing and everybody's a part of it. There were the workers, there were the really skilful players and there were the match winners. Maybe two thirds of a good side are workers, they'll tackle everything, take the ball up and back up when they can. The other ones can run round 10 players, sidestep three and score under the posts. They were the difference makers, but everybody worked together. The difference makers got paid a bit more dough though.

Before John Monie left the club, he asked me did I want to take over? I said I had a testimonial coming up, they granted it to me for 12 months. I told them though that I didn't want to be in people's pockets for 12 months so I'd just take six. I'd like to thank the people who worked so hard to make my Wigan testimonial such a success. The people who ran it did a great job. They were good friends.

John Dorahy got the coaching job before the start of the 1993–94 season. He was a really unusual fellow. He would take a squad of around 21 players for the first team and none of them would be allowed to play 'A' team. With what was left, he said the academy would take the priority so I had the players in the middle. Then he told me he didn't want me coming on the coach to first team games. He must have thought I was a threat to him. I just told him if that was what he wanted, that was what we would do. I used go in the car to first team games. It would be amazing watching players come off the coach at first team games because four of them wouldn't be playing. Dorahy would only name the 17 on the coach on the way to the game so it was all up in the air.

With Dorahy's selection processes that year, it meant I was down on numbers for the 'A' team. I hadn't planned to play that year but ended up having to. I remember we played Halifax away and some of the young players got killed playing against Brendan Hill. I thought "That's not going to happen again". I started playing with the team down the league table. By the end of the season, if Warrington had lost their last game by 20 points, we'd have won the league.

That's when Sean Long came in. I had no stand-off at the time and was playing Andy Johnson there. Andy had the ball glued to his hands, he just wouldn't let go of it, he'd show the ball as if he was going to pass but it never happened. I would scream "Pass the fucking thing."

I got on really well with the scouts such as Jacko, Peter Farrell, Jack Roden and Derek Standish. I told them all I needed a stand-off. Jacko said to me, "Sean Long's just come into the academy and they won't use him because they want a big stand-off." I asked what he was like and was told he was a good stand-off. I decided to bring him into the 'A' team and give him a shot. He just slotted into the back line like a natural. He came in like another Shaun Edwards, he let the ball go, but could also do his own thing. He was a team man like Shaun. I thought "this will do me."

There was a lot of controversy surrounding Dorahy and after the Challenge Cup Final at Wembley the club sacked him. They came to me and asked if I would do the job temporarily and I agreed. It was almost the end of the season, but coming up very soon was a World Club Challenge match in Brisbane against the Broncos.

76

Avoiding a tackle against Castleford on 7 April 1991, Graeme's last first team league match for Wigan.

Scoring under the posts. (Courtesy *Wigan Observer*)

More silverware for Wigan – holding the Locker Cup.
Wigan used to play Warrington for this trophy as a pre-season match.

8. Coaching Wigan

I thought that Dorahy had restricted what players could do, he had treated some players differently, he tried changing the whole system. But in my opinion it didn't need changing, it just needed him putting his imprint on it. It just needed amending in small ways to push it forward. I thought at times that what he tried didn't work and I think he got frustrated with things not going right.

Initially, they asked me to do the first team job on a temporary basis. Ken Winstanley, a friend of mine and president of my testimonial committee, told me when I took the job, "Look Westy, you don't really want this job. These fellows have done everything. You can't do any better."

I told him, "I know you really well Ken, you're a great bloke, but I'm gonna give it a shot anyway." We both laughed at the end of it and celebrated a fantastic season. He was only trying to look out for my future in the game. I appreciated it, but I knew it was time for me to give it a shot.

I'd seen the team improve under the different coaches Wigan had over the years, but I'd seen it drop back a bit under Dorahy. All I needed to do was step it up again. When I took over, I thought Dorahy had put one or two good things in place, but had suppressed the player's freedom a wee bit.

He had gone for Va'aiga 'Inga' Tuigamala and chosen him over Jason Robinson. Now, it was a tough decision, but Inga didn't seem to be fully fit. I would have gone with Jason who had been playing brilliantly. Tuigamala ended up with a winners' medal at Wembley. Jason instead was playing in the 'A' team for me, and scored three tries in the game before Wembley. Neil Cowie joined Jason in not being selected for the Challenge Cup Final. When Dorahy got the sack, I brought both players back in. I went in and slotted things back together. Inga had been playing well on the wing, but I thought was a bit overweight. I'd had Jason Robinson on the wing for me in the 'A' team and he was killing them. I thought at the time that Jason was a better prospect because he had always played rugby league, he was as fit as a buck rat and he was playing to a high standard. Inga had come in from rugby union and I thought wasn't quite fit enough.

I spoke to Inga and explained that the team needed to go forward. I said that if he was carrying an injury, he was better not playing because it would set him back. I put Jason in for that first Premiership game against St Helens and he killed them. I thought "Thank Christ for that".

I had a chat with 'Giz' – Shaun Edwards – and the players went out to train, but Inga was in the treatment room. He told me his leg wasn't right so I put Jason in instead. We went through and won the Premiership.

We then went over to Brisbane for the World Club Challenge. Frano Botica was there to play the game but was umming and aahing about playing the next season because he said he was starting a business and going back to New Zealand. He was into everything. While he was still playing, he got into selling Amway cleaning products. Then he opened a bar in one of the islands with one of his uncles. I thought he was a bit of a wheeler-dealer, but a nice guy. We used to go round to see him, Tracy and the kids. His brother-in-law was over here as a chiropractor in Wigan. Tracy's mum and dad came over too. Her dad was a former policeman, Merv Kenny, and was coaching rugby union. I wanted Frano to stay, but he ended up leaving the club.

Dean Bell and Andy Platt had agree to join Auckland Warriors so did not play in the World Club Challenge. I understood why they didn't play. I wasn't disappointed; they had made their decision to go to Auckland and wanted a bit of time off. This game was another week into the off season. They had won the Premiership and wanted to move to New Zealand and their new club. They probably wanted a month or so off to take it easy. They had both played a great role in that year and in the Premiership win.

Things, at that stage, were conspiring against us. It was a challenge and we had to go over and play the game. Kelvin Skerrett had broken his jaw in the Premiership Final against Castleford at Old Trafford. Martin Dermott and Barrie-Jon Mather were carrying injuries. They were all up for it though and wanted to do it. I asked Billy McGinty if he would play prop and he said, "Yeah" even though he hadn't played for most of the year.

Nobody gave us a chance, especially the Australian media. Once again though, before the game I made a call that I had been mulling over in my mind for a while. With the way that things had gone under

John Dorahy, although the team had won the league and the Challenge Cup, they were under a bit of pressure. They were trying to play well, but it wasn't working as it should. We got to Brisbane and had a training session on the Thursday when I trained with the players. We had a gym session and a bit of a run around. On the Friday, they had a good session. I got all the players in and I had not told anyone, not even the directors, but I told them, "Right, you've got two days off. You've had a tough year and I can't make you any fitter. What I can do is take the pressure off a little bit. If you want to go and visit family or friends for a couple of days or whatever, go and do it."

When I gave them two days off, the directors looked at me as if I was mad, the players looked at me and started smiling but it all came together. They went out and Christ, they were everywhere. One player came into the hotel at six o'clock one morning. I went for a run one morning at 8 o'clock along the beach. Jack Robinson collared me: "Westy, what's this about someone coming in at six in the morning?"

I said, "Jack, leave them alone, I've told them they can have two days off."

I thought: "If we lose this game my coaching career is well down the tubes." We got to the Sunday night training session and I had told them before they left that the only thing I had wanted in response was the best training session they could give me. We trained under the floodlights at the Seagulls club. Shaun Edwards was captain; he called all the players together and said: "Those other coaches would have had us locked away; we'd have been bored to tears. He's let us go out for a couple of nights. We've come in here, we're all full of ourselves, telling each other what we've been up to and having a laugh. Let's get out and repay him."

I tell you what; all I did that night was say: "Start here." They were all flying that night. It was unbelievably good and the next two training sessions were the same.

The final session was a video session that I had put together on the way Brisbane played. I then got up and they were expecting me to give a Winston Churchill type speech. I just said, "Listen, you've done everything, I can't do much more, I can't tell you what to do, that training session spoke wonders, let's get out there and do the job."

They all looked at each other as if to say "Where's the speech?" They got up, filed out and away they went.

They repaid me for the days off in the training sessions and it carried over into the game itself. Players like Billy McGinty, Martin Dermott and Barrie-Jon Mather wanted to be a part of it and wanted to go out there and do their best. They did bloody well and then the players on the bench who came on went on and took it forward.

Dermott was injured, but went out and did his best until we replaced him with Martin Hall. Barrie-Jon Mather was injured too but went out and gave it his best shot until we replaced him with Paul Atcheson. Billy McGinty played outstandingly well. The team did the job for me and the club.

I had put Inga on the bench for the game. I didn't use him during the game because it was 20–14 and I looked at it thinking "Where can I put him?" He'd only played on the wing and I had Offiah and Robinson on the wings, two world class wingers. I thought it would be unfair on him to put him on with 15 minutes left because if he made a mistake and we lost the game he would take a lot of criticism. I always thought there were better things to come from him. At the end of the game I explained why I hadn't brought him on.

We won the game in front of over 54,000 Australians and it was bloody marvellous. I didn't really expect the result. It was some start to my coaching career, winning the Premiership and beating Brisbane in their own back yard, but that Wigan team had good players. They had proved they were great before and they knew how to play the game. It was just a case of gaining an understanding. I had to look at them individually and assess when somebody was overdoing it.

One example was Gary Connolly, he would train the house down. He was magnificent. I don't want to single anyone out because they were all great players. Gary would train hard then go and get battered in games; he would tackle everything and take the ball up. We had a chart at the club showing how everyone was performing on weights and so on. I would notice that Gary's performance had started to dip a bit. I'd go and see him on the Tuesday night when he'd be on the physio's table. I'd tell him to take the night off and he'd argue, "No, I'll train, I'll train". I would eventually persuade him to take the night off and ease off a little bit. He'd come back in on the Thursday and then I'd tell him to take it easy and not overdo it. It was just to try and freshen him up.

Gary Connolly was one of the players I was in awe of really. Like Henry Paul, I would see him do things on the park that I didn't see other people do. When I first saw him play full-back for St Helens, he was under a lot of pressure as a kid. He didn't get much in the way of protection under the high ball. People could see there was something there but it wasn't going to come out in those circumstances. Johnny Jackson, our scout, was from St Helens and he knew what Gary was capable of doing. He helped bring Gary to Wigan. When I got to coach Gary, gee he was unbelievable. He trained harder than anybody. If he enjoyed a beer and played like that, that was fine by me. Gary liked his social life. I was the same; I would enjoy a beer after the game on a Sunday and forget about it for awhile. Gary was a great player and he would be in my team any day. It showed in his longevity, he played rugby union later in his career and he carried on playing until he didn't want to play anymore.

Once we were playing Bradford. They were attacking with three men, Gary was our sole defender. He hit the player with the ball, picked it up and next thing we were attacking down the other end. Unbelievable. When he later went to play an off season in rugby union in 1996, he would come up to Wigan during the week to get in the weights room. It was surprising. I knew Henry and Jason would be the same, the one I had to worry about was Inga. He would come back fit, but not fit enough for rugby league.

Inga was going back to New Zealand for a month after the World Club Challenge so I told him to go over there, enjoy himself. When he came back though, I had some plans for him. While he was over there, I got a call from someone saying, "Inga's not right for a Graeme West team?"

"You are bloody kidding," I replied. "We've just organised a game for him especially so he can play at centre. A few of us think he can play there so we've arranged a pre-season game for him to play there, he just has to get fit." That's what we had done with Nigel Wright at stand-off.

Inga came back, he ran all over Haigh Hall. He worked really hard. I have to take my hat off to him, he lost a stone and a half. He was on fire and it was all down to Chris Butler, the conditioner. Give Inga his due though, he stuck with the training, even though he hated it.

I had formulated a plan. Dean Bell had gone, we were short of a centre and I saw Inga's future there. He had the size and the ability to play there. He never looked back once the season started and it was down to him. He made the commitment to do it. There were other players who didn't.

I tried to get a bit of weight off one of our forwards because at that time there were only two subs in the game, and I thought he wasn't fit enough. If we had a couple of injuries and he came on, we were short of a player. I just couldn't get the weight off him. Inga did it and I was very proud of him. I remember when Inga went up to Newcastle to play rugby union. A mate of mine's son was playing for Newcastle at the time so I went up to watch a couple of games. I spoke to Inga and he said: "Come and meet our conditioner". The Newcastle conditioner was a big bloke. "This is the best conditioner I've ever had," Inga said. I looked at Inga and thought "You've got him under the thumb haven't you." He had put at least a stone back on. Inga had been able to cajole and bullshit this conditioner. He couldn't do that with Chris.

I went over to New Zealand recently and saw Inga and he told me that he felt he had never really thanked me enough for what I had done for him. I told him that he had done all the work with the help of Chris Butler. Just the mention of Chris's name sent Inga into growls. He then said: "I never thanked him either, I should have done." I just told him that at the time he had been too busy trying to kill him.

It was great that people like Chris Butler would come and chat with me about players and future games that we had coming up. We'd look at a tough game we'd have coming up in three weeks and knew that we had to do the hard work in training now. The week after would be a couple of hard sessions, then ease it down in the week of the game. It worked because we would see the players freshen up before key games. Individually, it was about looking at players and seeing when they weren't playing so well. I'd have a chat with the players concerned privately and ask them what the matter was. I'd tell them that the next game I would be putting them on the bench.

"Why?" would come the reply because they were all dying to play. I would explain they needed to freshen up, get their game right and that their game had sort of flattened out a bit. They would try and protest that they would be ok. I would explain that I would be giving a younger player a chance and some experience: "He's playing really well in the 'A' team," I would say.

"No, I'll be right, I'll be right," would come the somewhat panicky reply. Come the game, the young player would go out trying to impress then I'd put the older player on and he'd be ripping it up, killing everybody. It was one of the things I did that really worked.

One of the rules I had was if a player had been playing well and got injured so had to miss a match, it was understood that when he was fit to play he would go straight back into the team. The young player who had been filling in would come back out. That was understood by the young player as well. They knew though that if they played well, dropped back down into the 'A' team and kept playing well that if the first team player dropped his form they would be back up. We were always putting a little bit of pressure on players so they were looking over their shoulder: "If I don't do my job that kid's going to take my place" and so on.

The young players coming through, like today at Wigan, had to have the insight into how to approach being a first team player. It kept pushing the side forward. It goes back to when I was 'A' team coach, the first team coach, one of the directors and the rest of the coaching staff would sit down with a big chart on the wall that would list first teamers, 'A' teamers, academy players and players who had been signed. We would decide between us which players would go into which list. We'd plan it all out and work out who was going to take whose place when players left at the end of a season and where to put players whose form wasn't so good. We would always be planning for the future and players would either get a tick, a cross or a question mark. Everyone's opinions were taken into account. The player's rating could change the next month when we would repeat the exercise.

I didn't have any issues with managing the big personalities in the first team dressing room. I had a lot of help from what the previous regimes had put in place. There was a lot of professionalism and a good work ethic. There were players who might not like each other so much, but they were there to do a job to the best of their ability. Not to be detrimental to any of them, but the hub of it was Shaun Edwards. He was the pivot between the forwards and the backs. Now, if a winger or centre doesn't get good early ball they're not going to be able to score a try. Shaun would see the opportunity for them to score. The forwards would be led by the hooker, which would be Martin Dermott or Martin Hall.

I used to run the Graeme West Summer School and I still get people coming up to me today who say that they attended and had a great time. We used to run it in conjunction with Mick Hannon of Robin Park. It would run for a week and we'd have kids coming from everywhere. All the players would come down too. Each of the players would take a group after being given handouts of what I wanted them to do. The kids would swap groups throughout the week so they'd each get a turn with all the players. The players were good with it and responded well. A lot of the young players who eventually came through at Wigan were at those summer camps including Andy Farrell. He was playing at Orrell St James and was developing well anyway.

I used to go and watch a lot of games and would also rely on my scouts to recommend players to me. I always said that if someone wanted to do well, they had to be involved. We would have scouts all over the area, throughout St Helens and Warrington and so on. The scouts deserve the accolades for discovering the talent and the directors at the time for signing those players. Sometimes though, the directors got carried away and signed their own players.

The next season, 1994–95, we went through and won everything. One game we didn't win was at Halifax. I look back on it and think about what I could have done better. Traffic was pretty bad and we probably arrived a little bit late at the ground. We had arrived late at grounds before, but on that night, they just caught us cold. As coach, I was in charge of all the organisation so I look back and think I could have done better. We also lost to the Australian tourists 30–20 which was a good game. We got caught cold early in that game too. We built up momentum later on in the match so if we had held them early on, we might have beaten them. That was a great season and was the only time Wigan won everything they could.

When we did the clean sweep of all the trophies in 1994–95, there were some close calls along the way, but I always had confidence. The players I had were in the same boat as me, they had been in that situation before so many times. They had the ability to step up and do something. That's why we bought players of that quality. When there are players on the field such as Offiah, Edwards, Connolly, Tuigamala, Robinson and Paul they'll keep the ball moving until they find a gap.

When the gap comes, a coach can count on them to take the opportunity. Nine times out of ten that would happen.

The professionalism of the team was fantastic; we had won the league, but still had the Challenge Cup Final and Premiership to come. The team's aim was to win every game we had left that season. We'd offer players who had knocks a week off, but none of them wanted to miss out. They all wanted to be a part of winning every game. It was just a great attitude.

We went down to the BBC Sports Personality of the Year a number of times, and even won 'Team of the Year' in December 1994. We were the first rugby league team to win this award since it started in 1960. I got coach of the year at a Sky Sports awards ceremony. They had put us on a private plane to go down. Then I walked to the stage with Jon Bon Jovi. He was only a little fellow. They were all fantastic nights. We would talk to one or two people from other sports at the BBC events. It was a little easier for players such as Shaun Edwards and Martin Offiah to mingle as they did other work for the BBC and so knew more people there.

I got on ok with my fellow coaches, but even with John Monie when he had been at the club, I might have a beer with him after a game, but I wasn't acting like long lost buddies or any of that. It was a professional thing. I remember one incident with Doug Laughton. He had Kurt Sorenson playing for him at Widnes. They were coming over to play us and Laughton must have thought he could upset the apple cart. The morning of the game he put in the paper that Wigan were after Kurt and that I might be headed there in exchange. I thought "I'll have the bastard after the game." We went out and won the game. Afterwards I told Laughton, "Hey, that's enough of that. Don't be messing around with me in the papers."

In April 1995 there was the announcement that Super League was going to be set up in Great Britain and Australia. It split the game because some players and clubs were staying loyal to the ARL in Australia. Thus, before the 1995 Wembley final, all the players were up and down the stairs going to talk to the directors. We would be training and players would be organising Super League or ARL contracts. It didn't really involve me as the coach. I realised that the players had to do what was right for them and if it needed to be done at that particular time, it needed to be done. We still completed our training and won the final, beating Leeds, but it was a bit of a disruption. They were thinking about their careers though and it was really important to them.

Leading the team out at Wembley against Leeds as coach was great. It was like being in paradise. After each Wembley final, the Wigan players would smash up the dressing room at Central Park. I could never see the point in it myself. It was a traditional thing. I'm fairly certain the directors took it out of the players' winning pay to cover the damage. I don't think the players realised that.

Kris Radlinski – Rads – had never played for Wigan schoolboys, unlike the rest of the local players. I was quite amazed at that. He got a chance under John Dorahy. Unfortunately, Wigan got beaten quite heavily at Castleford when Kris was playing. It didn't work for him that day as it didn't work for many of them. The season we won everything, Rads was getting spells of one or two games. Before the Premiership Final, Inga had to go back to New Zealand because his grandfather had died. I asked one or two players their opinion and we put Rads in at centre. He scored three tries, the first time that had been done in a Premiership final, and got the Harry Sunderland Trophy. He really blossomed after that.

There were moves practiced at training that would work a treat on match day. When we had players like Giz, Henry Paul and Gary Connolly all working together, the gaps would just open up. Rads was a great young talent and he's still at the club now, on the coaching staff. He comes from a great Wigan family.

Martin Offiah was a hell of a talented player. I'd be hard pressed to select any other wingers in my team ahead of Martin and Jason Robinson. He was always a nice man with a great attitude. When Dorahy was coach, when the ball was kicked off into the corner, he had wanted Martin to take the ball up into the middle where the forwards were. I didn't see why Martin should have to take the ball up in those areas. When I became coach I told Martin that I didn't want him taking the ball up because that's what those ugly buggers called forwards do. I explained that when there was a break down his side of the field, his job was to finish it off for us. I said if he had to tackle someone who was making a break, that was fine but don't run it into the forward pack. I didn't want him to get injured and needed him on the wing to finish opportunities in open play.

With the Challenge Cup at Wembley in 1995.

Shaun Edwards was adept at seeing an area of the field that was blocked. He would notice that after a few good runs up the middle, the opposition would bring an extra man in to cover leaving a gap out wide. Shaun would then get the ball to that area for our players to take advantage. With the quality strike players we had running the angle so well, it was difficult for the opposition to stop it.

We would look at teams on video and notice how they lined up their marker defence at the play-the-ball. We would then devise ways of exploiting any weaknesses that we identified. It was satisfying because the players could see it and execute it on the park. That's what is frustrating when a coach works with players who just want to play off-the-cuff. They don't see that it is important to play with a little bit of structure to allow the players to use their vision to engineer ways of beating teams. I consider myself lucky to have worked with so many talented players at Wigan. The scouts and directors were good as well. The person who also unwittingly helped me was Dorahy. I thought that he didn't associate with the players. He didn't involve them in going forward together; rather I thought he tried to do it from the outside telling them what to do. As soon as things got back to the way they had used to be, when I took over, things went forward.

Kelvin Skerrett was an angry man; he was a real block in the scrum. We played St Helens and he had been sent off. He had been sin binned prior to the sending off and I hadn't thought there had been anything wrong with it. I felt that if he hadn't have been sin binned he wouldn't have later been sent off. He got a two match suspension and I decided that we would appeal against it. I went up to the appeal. There were three men behind the desk; a referee, a legal man and a former player.

"Mr Skerrett has been sent off…"

"Whoah, what about the sin binning?" I asked.

"We don't do sin binnings in here".

I asked was the sin binning on his record and they said that it was. I said that if it was on his record, they should be able to look at it.

"Well, we will then," came the reply.

I asked them whether they felt it should have been a sin binning, they said they would have a look at it and asked us to leave the room. We came back in.

"You're right," they said. "That was no sin binning, we'll expunge it from the record, now we want to look at the sending off."

I explained that if the sin binning hadn't have happened, the sending off wouldn't have occurred.

"No, we don't look at it that way; we look at the incidents themselves."

I gave them the spiel and they agreed to take my views into account. They then asked to see Kelvin's record. He pulled this bit of paper out and it went from his arm and rolled down to the floor it was that long. I looked at it and thought, "Jesus, we're up against it here Kel". They sent us out of the room again and when we re-entered they told us the suspension stood. I felt like diving across the desk and giving them what for.

We went over to Dublin for another Charity Shield match in August 1995. When we got to the hotel, one of my jobs as coach was to make sure everybody was set up right. I made sure everybody had a bed then realised, "Where's my bed?" I asked the hotel staff and they said the only room left was in the gateman's house down the road. I thought "I'm not having that" and went and kicked one of the substitute players out of his bed and told him he was down the road. I explained to him that I had already done my apprenticeship and now he had to do his. I ended up sharing a room with Taffy the kitman. I was good mates with him. I was in the bed nearest the door and I hear this growling and shouts of "No you're not" and "Yeah I am". I walked across to the room where the noise was coming from and it was Martin Hall and Kelvin Skerrett having an argument over who would get the biggest bed in the room. There was a third, younger player in the room watching this with his eyes wide open.

"What's going on?" I enquired.

"I'm having the bed, he's not."

"I'm having it, I'm the prop."

After they both were totally knackered, Kelvin Skerrett got the bed, Martin Hall got the next bed and the young player got the couch bed.

It was a big, old hotel about 25 miles outside of Dublin. There were antiques all over the place and when I saw them I thought "This is a bit of a place to bring a rugby team". To be fair, the players were great. There was only one television set in the place so if someone cornered it, you were out of luck. The players ended up playing hide and seek or tick. I left them to it. Afterwards, they went outside kicking a ball around and lost two balls way up in the treetops. Taffy went mad at them for losing balls.

I later went back to Ireland, but this time to Belfast. One of my taxi mates used to be in the army over there. He married a girl over there and her family were intertwined with all different types of people. We went over there for a long weekend and a good look around. I'd heard these things on the radio such as 'the Falls Road'. We also had a look at where Martin McGuinness was supposed to have lived. We were invited to a pub and there was a camera at the door. We went through the first door and then there was another door with another camera. Finally, we were in the pub and it was like being on the waterfront with all the pirates. It was great though and they were really good people. We had a laugh and a few beers. I looked around and there were bars all over the windows. I could easily imagine what it had been like when times had been really bad where people could turn up with a petrol bomb. I loved Belfast.

One of the people who had made some of the woodwork on the beautiful Central pubs took us for a meal and it was fantastic. In one pub, a fellow walked in with a limp, I was told, "They got him". It's one thing being in a pub when a fight starts, but to be nabbed, taken outside and kneecapped is something else.

One player was the bane of my bloody life. He was cantankerous. He was always moaning and asking: "Why have we got to do this?" There was one stage where he was weight training outside the club. He knew one of the directors and used this so that he could sometimes get his own way. I remember in the build up to me being sacked I was told that my weight trainer was no good. This was after the season where we had only lost two games. I told them there was nothing wrong with the weight trainer. I said that at the end of the weight trainer's contract we could review things and if we wanted to, renew it. The director told me that the guy who was training this player had made him the strongest he had ever been. I replied that he was strong and big, but he couldn't get round the field. He was like a robot. The director repeated how strong this player was and that we should change the weight trainer. My view was that our weight trainer was tried and tested whereas I felt the player's trainer had made him cumbersome. I told the player that he had to weight train at the club and he wasn't happy about it. Not long after this conversation, the director came down shouting, "What's going on?" That's the way it was. Many years after this, I saw this player one night when I was out. He said to me: "You were right you know, I lost a stone and I felt twice as good getting around the park." One thing I will give him is that he played some great games. The best game I ever saw him play was the World Club Challenge. He played exceptionally well and I took my hat off to him. If he hadn't have got involved with that weight trainer and grown so big he would have been a lot better.

Jason Robinson is a great little guy. He spent very little time in either the academy or the 'A' team. He came in as a half-back, I asked him about playing half-back for me in the 'A' team and he told me he didn't really want to play in that position. I could see that his passing, while good, wasn't exceptional for a half-back. However, he played for the 'A' team a few times at half-back and did really well. He was rushed straight through to play on the wing in the first team. He took it by fire. As a young player, he did some of the things that young players do. At the same time, he did everything requested of him and did his work well. Inga had taken him to the church and Jason came into the changing room to speak to me. He said to me, "I'm not sure about this God you know. I'm not sure about this religion."

I said, "Look Jason, I'll give you one bit of advice. I like to bring my family up with all the right attitudes and to do the right things in life. I don't need to go to church to prove that. I like to have the same standards in life. You've got to make that decision, not me."

Away he went and he started going to the church with Inga, it was good for him. It focussed him on a different thing in life. He was always a great young man.

Squeezed into a go-kart with former Liverpool football star Ian St John ready to give me a push. (Courtesy *Wigan Observer*)

9. Super League … and rugby union

Obviously at Wigan, we had a number of star players in the ranks. One was Sam Panapa, who is a good mate. I went back to see him two years ago when he was moving to Brisbane. I went to visit him there and he was on his own. I had just caught him. He had only flown in 12 hours before us. We ended up staying with Maryann's niece who as luck would have it was staying just around the corner. Sam and Roz are great people with immaculate kids, a lovely family. His son ended up in one of the feeder teams for the Brisbane Broncos. When I have been back to New Zealand in recent years I go and see Howie Tamati, I've been to see Inga recently and Danny Campbell. I keep in touch with as many of them as I can.

Sam got on well with Chris Butler, our conditioner. He used to go running with Chris and do everything he needed to do to stay up there. Sam was a really good player who was exceptional when he needed to be. More than anything, he was a real block there, a solid rock in that area where he was going to go out and give us a good performance. He had a great career at Wigan and, in the end, he could play in a number of positions. I think what the directors thought was that he needed to move on so that some young players could come into those positions. We sort of felt the same, but what I wanted to do was to give him the academy coaching job. I was told that Sam was my mate and they didn't give jobs to people "Just because they're a mate." I told them that it was nothing to do with that and I was mates with everybody at the club, including the director I was talking to. I tried to be sociable with everybody, even the people I didn't like so much. I thought by giving Sam the job it would have helped us take a step forward. It wasn't to be.

Paul Atcheson, or 'Patch' as he was called, was another great young fellow. He worked really hard and was a big part of the team. However, a full-back can get left exposed and he got exposed a couple of times. Overall, he was a hell of an asset to the team. He was another one who came in from St Helens and moved on in the end. I've seen him since leaving the club and he is still the same bloke, he has the same great attitude. I like him.

Simon Haughton came to the club as a young player who worked very hard on the weights and his fitness. He became really big and strong. As other clubs' players hadn't done the work on weights that we were doing, he would just run straight through them and score tries. He went on to do it in the first team, but then the opposition got used to him. I thought what Simon didn't push on with was his handling. Other sides started coming up to the same levels of strength as Simon and he needed to come up with something else.

We would sometimes watch tapes and engineer moves. There were people we would talk to such as Jackie Edwards, Shaun's dad. He was great for letting us know what the opposition were doing. We would take things on board from people, players and even spectators. We would listen to what they had to say. I would never pooh pooh anybody, if it was no good, I just put it in the bin, but I held onto the good stuff.

Martin Hall was a player who would play anytime, anywhere for us. I loved him as a player. During the time Dorahy was coach, Martin Dermott dislocated his elbow. Dermott was another great, young Wigan player. When I took over as coach, Martin Hall got an extended run in the first team. He was like Gary Connolly in that he just wanted to get out there and play. I'd tell Martin that I thought he could snaffle a couple of tries. Once he had passed to the forwards, he just needed to follow up on the inside backing up. He had to get there anyway to be ready at dummy half. He started to score more tries. Martin Dermott came back and played in the 'A' team, he just couldn't displace Martin Hall. It was difficult as Dermott had played so well before, but Hall had a stranglehold on the position. In the end, Martin Dermott left the club.

Terry O'Connor used to come over from Widnes and I'd always see him sitting in our 'A' team changing room. I used to ask him what he was doing here and wasn't he supposed to be playing for Salford? He said he was, but didn't seem too thrilled about it. When he came to Wigan, he was an inspired signing. He worked really hard at his game. Once I was picking a team for a final, Terry had been playing out of his skin, but Neil Cowie just pipped him by doing it over a longer term. I had to go with Neil. I called Terry in and explained he was just a tiny bit away but, being straight with him, he wasn't going to be in the side. I told him he would be coming along as 18th man. I said that if he kept going the way he was, there would be more finals and he would get his chance. Lo and behold, the next final came and he was in. We won it; he was cheering and going, "Yeah, you were right."

"Well you've done your job, you've done the work. You could have taken your ball home and said you were better than that," I said.

Instead he had taken it on the chin and was able to reap the rewards. Look at how many finals he got in after that. He's another one with a great attitude who wanted to do well. He's jovial and has a laugh, but he's intelligent too. He could read a game, do the job and fit into a team environment.

When I was first team coach at Wigan, we needed a new reserve team coach. There was the suggestion that John Pendlebury come in to do the job and I remarked that I thought he was very opinionated, but that he worked really hard towards his goals. I had a meeting with him and told him we wanted him for the job, but everybody had to get in and pull the same way. He said that was fine, he came in and he was great. He kept promoting the young players and giving them a chance.

There was then a shortened Centenary Season from August 1995 to the end of January 1996 before the game switched to a summer season and Super League. We again won the league and beat St Helens in the Regal Trophy Final 25–16. There was only a short break before the 1996 season started.

The club's historic run of success in the Challenge Cup came to an end at the Willows in February 1996. We scored two tries early in that game that were both brought back for forward passes. Although I think they were both fair tries, we should have had the ability to accept those decisions and win the game. I also look back at myself and wonder if I selected the wrong team for that match against Salford. Other penalties were awarded at certain times during that match that also put us further back. Frustration started to creep in and at the end, we got beat.

I've always believed through my coaching career that my teams have got to go out and overcome any decisions from the referees as well as the opposing team. It meant we had to do everything exceptionally well. Salford won 26–16, our first Challenge Cup defeat since 1987.

For the inaugural Super League season, John Pendlebury and the conditioners put a lot of work into Scott Quinnell, everybody did. He'd joined us in September 1994 from Welsh rugby union. He could have turned into a hell of a rugby league player. I always believed if he hadn't have been sold, we'd have won that first Super League season.

He could have had a fantastic rugby league career, but he had to do what was best for him and he returned to rugby union. The club at the time needed that input of cash. It was disappointing though after bringing him in with such a fanfare and working so hard on him that he was allowed to leave. I believe it's true that Joe Lydon came up with the nickname 'Foo' for Quinnell. He was a bit of a character; Joe. He was good to have around.

We played Bath in a two leg cross-code challenge in May 1996. Shaun Edwards was upset we didn't get 100 in the first leg, which was played under rugby league rules. We beat them 82–6 at Manchester City's Maine Road ground. At the time, rugby union players weren't fit and were used to playing a dour, strangling game. They would trundle around the park and to play an open game against us, I knew it would be far beyond them. I didn't realise how much beyond them it was though. We destroyed them in the first half. I went down at half time and spoke to the Bath coaching staff. I said: "Listen, don't take any notice of the rules. I will speak to the referee and you can have unlimited interchanges in the second half." For my part, I took off Edwards, Tuigamala and Farrell. I just wanted to try and even it up a bit. They were all demanding to go back on. I just had to tell them to leave it. Shaun was so competitive and wanted to show how strong we were. I thought though there's rubbing someone's nose in it and then there's taking the piss.

The other thing was we had a Super League game at the weekend and I wanted my best players to be fresh. We had to play all the regular league games plus the Bath games and the Middlesex Sevens as well. That meant fitting in rugby union training sessions. It was a bit of a distraction, but it was also a challenge. There was money to be made, games to be played and we wanted to be a part of it. It was a time of big change in both codes of rugby.

The Middlesex Sevens at Twickenham was fun. We went out to do a training session in the car park and all the cars parked around us, they'd be having their pâté and wine out the back of their Range Rovers. A few of them had to get out of the way because we were spraying the ball around. All the spectators seemed to be outside. Then when it was time for us to play, the pâté was put away and the spectators headed to their seats to watch us. It was packed every time we played. We got to the final and Wasps scored. The crowd started to sing *Swing low sweet chariot*. I thought "Fuck you too". Away we went, we blitzed them. We ended up giving them a bit of a smacked arse and won 38–15. All the way through, we had to look at the challenge in front of us, how can we be better? We had to look at the people around us; we had to look at the organisation as a whole. A coach should be always looking at ways things can be done better.

I played in the union leg of the Bath games in the back-row at the age of 43. I'd been playing veteran rugby union with Joe Lydon. Some of our young players hadn't played any union and the thought was if I could play for a certain amount of time, it would take the sting out of it a bit for them. I thought that was fair and also didn't want any injuries with the rest of the league campaign still ahead of us. I'm always up for a game. I played until just after half time and told them I'd had enough. My neck was killing me and it took about three months for it to be right again. Terry O'Connor and Neil Cowie would be jumping up in the scrum and coming down on my neck. In the end we lost 44–19, but scored a couple of good tries.

Jeremy Guscott refused to take part in the games. That was his choice. From my point of view, it's about competition. There are people in other sports who are written up to be great players. We wanted to compete against them and we wanted to compare ourselves against them.

Our players were all competitors and had a great attitude. We would have really tough training sessions and when I was coach I'd put an indoor basketball court in the gym. Some of the players loved playing basketball.

After a tough training session, Inga, Henry Paul, Jason Robinson and sometimes Shaun would go on the court and try and keep the ball off the ground while only taking two steps. They would be ducking, diving and laughing. It was just pleasure to them. They were advancing their skill levels, but they were also having a bit of fun. They used to love playing with the ball. There were other days where we would play two on two on that court or everyone, including the coaches, would take free shots at the basket to see who would brew up. As soon as I left, Eric Hughes took that court down. I always thought with something like that, it was good to see players with a smile on their face.

Inga took me by surprise once, he and I stayed behind after training for a session in the gym. We were in the shower and he said, "Westy, can you do me a favour?" I said I would.

"Can you not blaspheme so much in your team talk?"

"Shit," I said. "Sorry about that, I'll try my best to do that for you."

The next two games we won well and I was pleased with myself for watching my language with the team. The next game, the opposition scored just before half time and I came into the dressing room with a, "What the fucking hell is going on?" I looked around to see Inga shaking his head. He waited until all the other players had gone out and said, "Westy, you owe that swear bottle some money you know."

The match that ultimately cost us the league in 1996 was a home draw against the London Broncos. I thought that they were allowed to lie on us throughout the game and really slow us down. We got frustrated that day because in all the games leading up to it, such lying on hadn't been allowed. I told the players at half time to be patient and keep working. By lying all over us, London were able to get their defensive line set. They slowed the game down to their pace. We couldn't engineer a gap because we'd been used to quick play-the-balls. It happened a few times; we went to Leeds, Gary Connolly tackled a player, bounced back up and was penalised for lying on.

I was getting frustrated as a coach due to the referees' lack of consistency, one week players could lie all over the man, the next they had to be off within a second. I would write reports to the referees and try talking to them, but it was like talking to a brick wall. Sometimes I thought the referees were trying to test us. There was a time in the 'A' team we played Hull KR under a certain ref. I had made the team practice going back a further half yard behind the ref for the game. I was playing, so I had to make the extra half yard as well. I pointed this out to team and added: "If an old git like me can do it, you young bucks can too." This referee was dying to penalise us but, thanks to the extra half yard, he couldn't. I was laughing at him in the end.

In 1996 I took the players to a health farm in Leicestershire. They each got two free treatments which could include a rub down. I had to get them all together and warn them, "Behave yourselves." Some of them were notorious for putting a towel round them with no underpants underneath to surprise the girls giving the treatments. Those sorts of trips were great to break up the monotony of training every week. It would shift their concentration too and give them something else to talk about. They would be laughing and giggling at different things that had gone on while we were away. The best players have to be good, but they have to be intelligent too. Players have to switch on to different teams they play and situations they face on the field. Players also have to be focussed on what they are doing. At the same time, every now and again, players have to be able to enjoy themselves. We'd find that some players may go for one or two beers during the week; others would see their parents or spend time with their mates. It was good for them to do something different and get away from rugby before coming back in the next day. If a few of them had done something together, for example a game of golf, they would all be laughing about it the next day. They would give each other stick over who played well and who was useless. It took the boredom out of things. That was one of the problems players faced on tour. After training, the players would spend a lot of time in their rooms. It was always good to have a day out or something, it created talking points.

As I said earlier, we could have won the first Super League in 1996. We lost to St Helens early in the season. Scott Quinnell was starting to come really good for us after about 18 months at the club. I played him against Saints at Central Park and he killed them. We smashed them all over the place. The next week, he was sold to the Richmond rugby union club. Skerrett and Cowie had long term injuries and I explained to the directors that we needed to bring in another prop. We only had Terry O'Connor at the time. I was told that the club had a prop in mind and that even if we needed to wait 12 months for him, he would be the one we would sign. I said we needed a prop now because in the remaining games we had to travel to Bradford and that was looking a bit dicey. I knew that without two props we would struggle at Odsal because they had a big, strong team. Joe Lydon sorted out a swap deal for one of our players to go to Leeds in exchange for Neil Harmon. The directors blocked the deal. We went to Bradford and played Terry O'Connor and Mick Cassidy at prop. We lost the game 20–12 and Saints went on to win the title by a point from us. I'm not saying that with Neil Harmon we'd have won Super League, but we'd have had a better chance of winning it. The prop the directors were going to sign the following year wasn't someone I felt was a top line player.

The team had a great belief in what they did. At the same time, we all knew the run of success Wigan had enjoyed would come to an end. Wigan supporters would say to me, "I've had enough, I'm not going today; they only need to turn up to win." I would reply, "Well it's your decision but I'll tell you one thing, it's not always going to be like that, if you want to enjoy it, enjoy it now. At some stage, it's going to go backwards either due to a decision or some financial problem."

It amazed me because, in my opinion, the directors ended up taking their eye off the ball. We may have contributed to it with some decisions, but the club did start to go backwards. Then I would hear supporters say, "We can't win anything, we're bloody rubbish." I would remind them that I remembered the years when we were winning everything and some people didn't want to go. A coach can't win with spectators sometimes. No team will win everything all the time. A coach needs a good work ethic and to be able to keep signing the right players. Over the years, the directors made some fantastic buys, but I think it got to the point where they thought they could sign ordinary players and we would make them into superstars. Maybe that was a financial issue, but it was never going to work. Maybe they could sign four cheaper players for the same price as two good ones. I would rather have the two good ones. Some of the players the directors brought in were potentially good, such as Tuigamala and Quinnell; they just needed to get fit. We did that and Scott would have become a great rugby league player while Inga was great.

Jack Robinson has had some misfortune over the last few years and I wish him all the best. I look back and see the amount of stress he was under. I would go to see him when he was chairman of Wigan and he would be holding a phone doing deals for players, I would come in to ask him something and he'd be buying furniture in for his business at the same time. It was too much and he was like that from morning to night. It was like Maurice Lindsay trying to be chairman of Wigan and chairman of Orrell Rugby Union club; I thought it was too much for one person. A coach or a director has to keep their eye on the ball at the thing they do. No one can do everything.

10. Widnes

The end of my time coaching the first team at Wigan was when the club started heading downwards. Towards the end, I think the director's eyes were taken off the ball in the struggle over who owned the club. They had gone over to New Zealand and bought players who weren't good enough. I got phone calls asking me, "What are you buying them for? They're not to your standard." I had to see what the hell was going on. The directors told me that they were good players and that I was too negative. The two players concerned were Doc Murray and Stuart Lester. Neither of them made much impact at the club. They weren't players we could really work with. During the off season, as well as signing two ordinary players, they let four players join rugby union clubs on short term contracts, namely Jason Robinson, Gary Connolly, Henry Paul and Va'aiga Tuigamala.

At the beginning of the 1997 season, the new players arrived and we had to face Saints in the Challenge Cup. Saints had prepared well, we hadn't. We had players just arriving at the club or just coming back and had only played one game which was against Chorley. We couldn't really have done much more because the players hadn't been there. Inga had come back from union not fit enough for rugby league and Gary Connolly had come back injured so couldn't play against Saints. We got beaten by Saints 26–12. They had a man sent off and still beat us. That was fair because they played better than us.

That was my last game in charge. It wasn't all my fault, but because I had taken the directors on about buying these players, they wanted me out. It was disappointing in one way, but because of what they were doing and the decisions they were making, I could see the club was starting to drop. I thought that if that was the way they wanted to take it, I really didn't want to be a part of that. It was hard because if they had made a couple of right decisions, they would have stayed at the top or thereabouts.

They told me they wanted to be football manager. I did not want to take that role because I could see the club sinking. I told them that they had had Joe Lydon in that position and it hadn't worked out. Joe tried hard and gave it his best shot, but I thought they didn't take the role seriously and they hadn't offered him a new contract. In my opinion, Joe hadn't been allowed to do any of the good stuff that he had tried to do; the directors just pooh poohed him. There was no chance I was ending up in the same position. They said, "You're too negative, we don't want you to coach anymore, we want you to be football manager." They then offered me the role of director of football. I told them I wouldn't do that either because I'd probably end up disagreeing with them. I had already been arguing with them as coach so I told them I was out of there. I said: "You don't want me to coach? Fine, sack me." I thought they were starting to make bad decisions. One example is Sean Long who was injured at the time, but was beginning to come right again at the start of 1997. After I got the bullet, the directors swapped Longy and £70,000 for Lee Hansen. That's Sean Long and £70,000 for Lee Hansen.

To be fair to the players who had been signed for that 1997 season, they went out and worked hard, but as the season went on, they were found to be just a little bit wanting. It also took the players who had been to rugby union a while to get up to speed again. That year, under Eric Hughes, they only won the Premiership at the end of the season. I was disappointed to leave, but took it on the chin. The hierarchy of the club and I had worked so hard to get it to a certain level. I knew, due to certain decisions, things weren't going to keep going. I just got on with life.

As well as selling Longy, the biggest thing that disappointed me was that Wigan let Shaun Edwards go. We would do hill running in training and nobody could keep up with him. He was the fittest player at the club. Offiah, Botica, Robinson, none of them could keep up with him. He used to lead everything and was fit as a buck rat. He wanted to go down to London to spend a few days with his son each week, but he'd have been back up to Wigan on the Wednesday and he'd have trained the house down. Look at what happened to Wigan after that with their half-backs. None of them came in and did any good. None of them were as commanding as Giz. He had great players around him, but he was a team half-back, he could use all those players around him. He was the lynchpin. If the winger was going to score a try, Shaun would see the opportunity first and give the winger early ball. Shaun was also a fantastic support player. He'd learnt that from Ellery who very often would wait in an offside position. They started catching on to Ellery after a while.

I always used to go to the gym at Wigan regularly because I worked in the pools office and was player-coach of the 'A' team. I would go into see who was in the gym; Faz and Cassidy would always be in there as would Forshaw and Gildart. The others would come in now and again. I would work out regularly in that gym. When I got sacked from Wigan, I knew I needed to keep going to a gym because it was part of my life. I didn't want my joints falling to bits and wanted to keep in reasonable nick. I had seen some players after they had finished playing become as fat as pigs. I thought that while I might get fat, I also wanted to be fit.

One of the people who had come down to our training sessions was a fitness fanatic called Royce Banks. He had a gym in Ince so I thought "Bugger it, I'll go down there". I went down there and there were some unbelievable characters.

Royce was into everything; especially wrestling and rowing. He got me into rowing. We used to try and do 2,000 metres as fast as possible on the rowing machine. We did a lot of practice for it so he organised a 'row off' against the top ten police rowers in Blackpool. Away we went with our ten and I did the 2,000 in six minutes 39 seconds. I was over the moon with that. We beat them. Royce would organise that sort of stuff. As time went on, Royce decided we would have a go at doing 100,000 metres. Again, there was a team of ten of us who would do the distance combined. The first time we did it, we would each do a stint of 250 metres. It was very hard work and took us over five hours to complete. We would get on, do our stint, get off, wait for the other nine to do theirs and then be back on again. When we got to 80,000, I thought that if I had to do many more 250 metre stints, I would die. Some of the others agreed so he cut the stints to 150 metres.

We ended up holding the world record for indoor rowing. As time went on, somebody beat the record. Royce decided we would do it again, but needed to go faster. We suggested doing the whole thing in 150 metre stints because we all felt more comfortable with that. We broke the world record again. Then Leander, Pinsent and Redgrave did it and smashed the world record. Royce said we would have another crack at it, I told them they could count me out this time. Undeterred, he got a team together and they retook the record once again. They put a fantastic team together, broke the record comfortably and still hold it. That was all part of the gym work down there.

At the gym trying to break the world indoor rowing record.

I would wrestle with Royce sometimes. He ran a Saturday afternoon wrestling session for about four years. He would hire a local church hall and sometimes only about three people would come down for it. New people would come in and give it a go, look at it and think "I've had enough of that" after a while. They'd come and go, but three or four of us were regulars. It was great, although eventually I had enough of that as well. Wrestling has long been connected with Wigan with the art of 'hooking' or 'shooting' well known throughout the world and its origins were in the town. Royce was very good at it; he is very fit and strong. He's a great character.

There are some great characters among the regulars there, always shouting for me to come and have a row with them. Two or three of the older fellows are always giving a lot of banter. I've pulled myself away from things that tie me down these days, I don't want to have to be there on a Saturday to wrestle. I just want to go down there when it suits me. There's a punch bag there I can bash, a dummy that I can throw around. There are runners and steppers. It's a great gym and it's the right price, I really enjoy going.

I stayed out of the game for three months before coaching Widnes for a while. Widnes weren't doing so well. A mate of mine was one of their scouts and he helped organise it for me to talk to the club. They rung up and I spoke to Jim Mills. It turned out they wanted me to be coach. They gave me a two year contract. I got there at the halfway through the season with the club wanting to go up from the First

106

Division. We won the first game, but some of the players they had at the club really needed to get some momentum going.

Widnes wanted a magician, not a coach. They had less money then they had ever had before, but wanted somebody to take them to the top. That's when I saw what directors who I thought weren't doing their job properly can do to a coach.

The first night I went to training, I went into the treatment room and it was packed. There were players everywhere. There were only a handful of players actually outside training. I thought "I've got to stop this." After everyone had gone I spoke to the physios and said: "Listen, these people in here are a waste of time. How many of them are really actually injured?"

"A third of them."

"That's fine, but what I need from you is to say what players are injured and what players can swim."

I told the players that from the next training session, I would there two hours earlier because there would be a swimming session over at the baths for the players who could swim but weren't training. The players all thought this was great. Then they got there. I made them work. They had an hour of agony because I didn't want them going there to piss about. The following training session, threequarters of them were on the training pitch.

When I was at Widnes, one of the directors came to see me and said there was psychologist who wanted to come in and speak to the players. I said to the director that I had seen psychologists before, but that he could come in and have a word because I was prepared to keep an open mind. The psychologist came in to speak to me and I said, "I've heard all of it before and it was bullshit. If you're going to come in with bullshit then it's going to have a negative effect." He told me that he had something that was really going to grab their attention. I told him that would be good and that I was prepared to try one session to see how it went.

He came in and addressed the players: "Right, psychology is the positive aspect of any game. You can't go out there thinking 'Look at the size of these lot, I'm going to get belted.' You've got to go out thinking 'They're going to get some today.' You've got to think that you're good enough and that you've trained together, all the positive aspects."

107

He had put that on the board then he wiped it off. He told the players to look under the bottom of their chairs because he had marked an 'X' on the bottom of one of the chairs. Whoever was sitting on that chair had to come up to the front and explain what he had just said. They all looked terrified while they checked to see if they had the 'X' on their chair.

He said, "Sorry, sorry, I'm fooling you, but how many of you thought 'I can't do that, I can't do that, I hope it's not me'." They all agreed that was the case and he said, "That's what I mean about positive, you needed to be thinking 'Right I'll get up and do it' that's what I mean about being positive."

He went on about the positive side of the game and what you can and can't do. He told everybody he would give us an example. He got the biggest prop in the room and got him to sit on a chair, he then asked for four volunteers. He asked them to put their hands out, put two fingers together in each corner of the chair and lift him off the ground. He told them to close their eyes while he told them they had had the best pre-season they have ever had, they were going to go out and run over hot coals, that they knew they had done all that weight training, just think about it. He then told them again he wanted them to go to the chair and lift him off the ground. They lifted him off the ground. We were all looking at each other thinking "Jesus".

The one that really got everybody was when he asked for another two volunteers for another demonstration. He got a steel rod, put a small piece of paper at either end so it wouldn't scratch the players then balanced it between both players' throats. He then took it out and put it on the table. He then told the two players that they were going to walk together with that steel rod pressing against their throats. Again, he gave them a motivational type speech. He put it between them, they walked around and the steel rod actually bent in the middle. He went to take it out, it sprung and hit him in the chops cutting him open. That wasn't meant to happen, but showed the tension the rod had been under. The players were amazed because they thought it would have gone through one of the player's throats. He just said, "That's what we're talking about, positive thought and positive actions, you can change things." It was a lot better than what I had previously experienced.

At Widnes at that time, we had good players, but they had limited ability in terms of intelligence and vision.

I actually lent the club £5,000 of my own dough to go towards the financial hole. There were about 10 directors at Widnes, I would go into the boardroom and everyone would be firing questions at me. I'd have thought they could have got their heads together and nominated one spokesman. Apparently, at the time, if you had £5,000 to put into the club you could be a director at Widnes. I thought "I could have been a director as well." It was a strange place to operate in. No wonder some clubs don't survive. A lot of club directors are businessmen, which is a little frightening. I sometimes wonder how the hell they run their businesses.

Longy was there. Now I had coached Longy in the 'A' team at Wigan. Great player and I thought Wigan would have kept him. When I went to Widnes, I could see the team needed something. Longy was helping them, but they needed more than him. Longy's style of play was great, he was the star, but with the right team around him I knew he would be a brilliant star. Soon after I joined the club, we knew we weren't going to be able to go up. David Howes was chief executive of St Helens at the time and he rung me up. He asked me what Longy was like and did I reckon he would suit Saints. I told him that Longy was made for them. I said he had everything you could want, he might be a bit unruly, but you can handle that. If you get into his head, you can manage that side of things.

There was a charity function for a young kid who had got hurt midway between Widnes and St Helens and we were all going. Jacko, the fellow who signed Longy for Wigan was with me at Widnes. I told Jacko to come with me to have a chat with David Howes. We chatted to Howes about all of Longy's attributes. He asked me how much we wanted for him and I told him, "£100,000".

"Jesus, that sounds a bit high," he said. "I'll go back to the club and see what I can do."

It couldn't have been a problem because Saints came back to us and did the deal for Longy for £100,000. So that makes Lee Hansen's valuation £170,000! No chance.

Longy was off like a shot and never looked back. It was great for him that he wasn't going to be at Widnes because the team wasn't there for him. To go to a team like Saints that would suit him down to the ground was just a dream move for him. He thanked me in his book for letting him leave Widnes, but there are no thanks necessary, it was just a natural progression. If I helped him along that's great. I liked him, even though he was an unruly bugger and I had to kick his arse at times. He was a great little player with tonnes of spirit. What I found with those little fellows is that they're playing among big blokes so they've got to be cheeky little buggers. Andy Gregory and Bobbie Goulding were the same. I had played alongside Bobbie and it was great playing with him. I would be fuming at the referee on the pitch and Bobbie would be shouting, "Westy, calm down" while I was growling away.

The players had to change their attitude a bit, they wouldn't change it before the end of that season and we didn't get promoted. The club started saying they were skint and had no money. At the end of that season, I was told that if the club didn't find some money, then they were going out of business because there was a 'big hole'. The £100,000 for Sean Long had obviously helped the club financially. I asked if half the money from the Long sale could be for new players.

"Sorry," came the answer, "it's all gone into the hole."

There was some money for signings and I managed to bring a couple of players in from Australia. We started the 1998 season and lost four games in the first eight league matches by less than four points. Later on they came to me and said I needed to take a pay cut. I replied: "Listen, you organised a two year deal and I've got nine months to go, when we get to the end of the deal we can negotiate."

They insisted they wanted me to take an immediate pay cut which I was unwilling to accept. I was told I had the next game to salvage my job. There was a clause in the contract allowing them to sack me if they gave me three months pay. We lost by two points and they told me I was down the road. I asked where my £5,000 was and they sounded surprised when I told them I hadn't received it yet. They gave me my money back and I was away. I'd been at the club for 15 months and left in August 1998.

Just after I went, the Bosman ruling came into effect which allowed free transfer of players when their contracts finished. I had been arranging for Widnes to sign Paul 'Buffer' Forber and half-back Mark Lee from Salford. They were prepared to join the club. I was down the road before I could do it. They would have been really good signings.

11. Motorways and Chorley

One of the Wigan directors, Arthur Thomas, had a motorway repair company. When I finished at Widnes, I decided I had to do something. He said he had a job going and I said, "Fair enough, I'll give it a shot." Ian Gildart came with me, we were a partnership on the motorways. It was brilliant, we had our own van and we'd take a young fellow with us, one of the apprentices. We'd go and do the job and we would have a great time. Our foreman would tell me and Gilly that he thought a particular job might have been done, but we were to go and check it had been and if it hadn't complete it. We'd go there, clean the job up and finish it off, have some lunch then sneak off to the gym. We'd get back to the depot around four o'clock because they wouldn't let you go any earlier. The foreman would say he had been to see us and where had we been? We'd claim we were up top. We would never stand on the motorway as it was too dangerous, we would go on one of the over roads. He'd say he hadn't seen us there either so we'd tell him we must have gone for a sandwich or something. He'd tell us we would have to be seen and I'd tell him that if the job was done, I would not be sitting on that motorway for anyone.

There were often rumblings of different clubs being interested me as a coach, but I learnt during my time at Widnes that travelling to places is not fun. I only lived in Wigan and believe me, getting to Widnes was a pain in the arse. There was no chance of me going anywhere further afield.

Maurice Lindsay went back to Wigan for about 10 years. I had a brief spell back at the club as the chief scout in 1999. During that time, there was a lot of change at the club. Dean Bell was brought in and was supposed to be in charge of player recruitment, but I don't know if he had the final say. He called me in and said: "In Leeds, Bob Tickles and I did it all. You've got about four scouts, they report to you and you report to me." I asked him if that was right but then thought I would just give it a shot and see how it goes. Wigan were under pressure at the time and weren't having that many good wins. Frank Endacott was coach at the time and we had a meeting with him one day. He told me that the players weren't performing and I suggested that he put one or two of the kids into the first team. I felt that he had nothing to lose because if those players caught fire, he would have another two players to choose from and also it would put pressure on the current first teamers to step up to the plate. He told me he couldn't do it because he was under too much pressure. I said that I was wasting my time being at the club because I was telling kids they had a shot at the first team, but if there was no chance they would wonder what I was on about.

Maurice Lindsay had done a great job for Wigan in the 1980s and early 1990s but when he went back in the 2000s he had to work within the salary cap. I thought that the club paid out too much money on just a few players. It meant that the rest of the squad was short. When they did put the kids in, they couldn't handle it and some got injured. They needed to be nurtured. He was used to the way he had done it in the 1980s and it didn't work out. That's why the club declined. I was always amazed how it was allowed to happen.

The Chorley coaching job came up and I took that for the 2001 season. I had always wanted the challenge of going to the bottom club that was getting kicked every week and see what I could do there. It was a personal challenge. I had a word with Peter Farrell; he agreed that it sounded good so he came with me. We went there for two years, he did the scouting and I did the coaching. Peter was great to work with. We got the club up from the bottom of the table as Lancashire Lynx to about third bottom in 2002. After those two years, I felt I had done my job and that it was time to move on.

A good signing I made at Chorley was when we pushed the boat out a bit and got Timmy Street. We stayed within our budget for the year though. He really lifted things for us.

People asked me was the gulf between Wigan and Chorley massive but they forget I had experienced similar circumstances coaching Wigan's 'A' team as well as back home in New Zealand. The players would train like hell, but some of them used to get on the piss on a Saturday night. They would work hard all week in their jobs so Friday and Saturday night was their chance to go out. We would have to drag some out of bed on a Sunday to come and play. I'd experienced both ends of the scale in that respect. It was just a matter of diversifying to a different sort of set up.

Once again, I had the situation where I was confined by directors that didn't really understand what was needed. Peter was the liaison with the board. The owner of the club, Trevor Hemmings, had a man who controlled the club for him. He was hard to deal with and I don't know whether he really wanted the job or not. He may not have fancied running a rugby team as well as his main job as head of one of Trevor's companies.

At one stage, all the pitches were frozen and we were looking for a place to train. Trevor Hemmings arrived in his Range Rover, picked us up and took us round his place. It was absolutely magnificent. He took us to where the horses trained on all-weather surfaces. He asked us whether this would help us, but I had to decline because the surface was too spongy. He told me if I needed anything to let him know.

Peter left the club as he had the opportunity to go to Saints as chief scout. I told him that he couldn't turn an opportunity like that down. At the end of the second year, I asked the directors what the budget would be for the following season. We had had a budget of £15,000 in the first year and then £22,000 in the second. I felt that if we could take that up to £28,000, we could kick on a bit more. I was told that a former director had sued the club for £20,000 so the budget wouldn't be as much. I countered by saying I was prepared to go out and organise sportsman's dinners and so on to raise some funds to make it up to the £28,000 mark.

Peter had already done some good work with Asda to get Sportsmatch funding. If we had put some money in, they would have doubled it as long as we did the promotion of Asda in the area. We needed to do some work to access the money and the directors told me they weren't prepared to organise it. I was frustrated because we had taken the club forward and just needed to do a little work to take it on further. I was prepared to do what it took, but the club structure wasn't there.

We had started doing some work with Runshaw College. They had a rugby league team and some of their players went out into the community as part of their job. They raised the game's profile in the schools. We went to train at the college. After the directors said they weren't prepared to do extra work, I told them that they should know early that come the end of the season, I would leave the club.

I wrote a report to Trevor Hemmings that I'm not sure he ever received, but it outlined that if we had just received another £6,000 on what we had received the year before we could have really kicked on. I left the club and Darren Abrams took the job. The club got the money from Asda and ended up with £50,000 to spend that season.   They got to second place in the league, which had now been split into two divisions, but went out in the first round of the play-offs. After another season, when they finished seventh, suddenly at the end of the 2004 season Chorley was no more. The club was bought by Blackpool, it was unbelievable. It had started to grow a little bit at a time and I look at what it could have become. It just wasn't to be. I felt that some of the directors just wanted to go down to the club on a Sunday and make sure the sandwiches were there. They would do their one sportsman's dinner a year, but weren't prepared to go above that. It sounds like I'm anti-director but I'm not. I don't make all the right decisions all the time, no way in the world. What I do though is think about my decisions before I make them.

When a coach goes to a new club, it has its nucleus of people there. They all stick together and they all have their ideas on how things should be done. A new coach tries to change things to be met with "You can't do that, we're used to doing it this way." The new coach has to try and change a whole system and culture. When a new coach goes into a club, he really needs to go in with his own backroom staff. Don't get me wrong, they were nice people at both Widnes and Chorley, but they weren't prepared to change.

When a coach has a player who doesn't want to stay at his club, it is better to get rid of him. It's no good having a discontented player hang around. The coach should get what he can for them and let them go. There's always another player out there somewhere. There was a player I had at Chorley who wanted to go to Leigh. I told the board to let him go, but they argued that he was one of our better players. I pointed out to them that if he didn't want to play for the club, it was a waste of time keeping him against his will.

After Chorley, my two boys were at St Judes and they were having problems with their coach. He was having a tough time with the team because they were a bit up-and-down and their attitude to training wasn't good. He was an outsider from St Pats and as I said before, clubs are very parochial. He was doing a good job, but it just sort of tore apart. Suddenly, they had no coach and asked me to do the job. Before I went to Chorley, I had previously coached there for a spell of around six months. I did the off season with them and the team went undefeated for nine games. When I went back this time, things were totally different. Half of them trained, half of them didn't. I thought I might have been able to swing it back round. The first year, I didn't think we were good enough to get promoted and finished 4th which I thought was good. After hard work in the next off season we did get promoted.

We had a good off season then, we won the first three games and I thought the players had started to look really professional. They just couldn't hold it though and started going down. People started crying off training and so on. It was like a slow puncture on a tyre, as soon as I started pumping it up, slowly it would deflate a bit somewhere. At the end of that season, I had kept them up but realised that with the players' attitude the most I could do with them is get them a third the way up the league. I had done three years so decided I was out of it.

I always believe in life that if you want to do something, do it well. You can't do it on your own, you've got to have people around you and you've got to have people you can talk to then come up with a consensus. A lot of rugby league isn't like that!

It is hard work, I've been to clubs that a coach can lift but then finds that he can't take them any further because they won't change that extra bit. That's when he thinks "There's no use me being here, they might as well have the dishwasher woman coaching them."

I'd had enough of the game at this point. I always believed as a coach and as a player if you're going to do something, you go out and give it your best shot. Your best shot comes from training in all the different areas of the game. Yes, you can have your good times, but you have to get the other areas right such as your attitude and your discipline. Above all, you needed to have the ability to see things at training or during a game and think "Right, we need to change something". The coach can give tips, but the player is the one who has to do out on the pitch. A lot of the players seem to think "She'll be right, we're doing alright".

It's great to see that Michael Maguire has come to Wigan now, put his foot down and changed the situation. He has said to the players, "You will perform or you will not be in the side". That should have happened years ago when Endacott was there, they should have give kids a chance. Brian Noble and Stuart Raper were the same. The club ended up selling loads of good, young English talent. Maguire has come in and changed it all. I would give accolades to the chairman too. He looked at Noble, felt that things weren't right and brought someone in to come and change it. It was a very disappointing time in Wigan's history that only ended when Maguire came over. The young players were not getting chances and in many cases were being sold. I would say to people, "They're never going to do any good until they put some young Wiganers in there, it just doesn't work." That's the case not just for us in the 1980s and 1990s, but also true throughout Wigan's history in the 1940s and 1960s. They had the guts to put young Wiganers in there. They're good enough, give them the time and they repay you.

I was invited into speak to the Wigan players before the first round of the 2010 Challenge Cup. I spoke to them about what the Challenge Cup means to Wiganers and some of the funny things that happened on the way through, I don't know if the coaches enjoyed those bits or not. In the end I said to them, "I must take my hat off to you and the coaching staff because over the last two years I didn't think this revival would ever happen, it's down to the regime the coaches have got and it's down to your work. You're looking far better than I ever thought you would and if you continue in the same vein, you'll do well in the future". I think they also invited Shaun Edwards and Andy Farrell.

12. Developing players

The hardest players to play against in my career were the ones who were organised. There might be a hard individual player who might give me a crack and be dirty. I knew I had a chance of getting them back. When I played a good team who were well organised, I couldn't get through their defence. That was the most frustrating. I would hit the ball right, step and they'd still be there. The Australians were always like that. From my first tour in 1975, their defensive line looked like a brick wall. They were everywhere and we realised we would really have to lift our standard to be able to engineer gaps to get half breaks and quick play-the-balls.

My favourite places to play were Central Park and Knowsley Road. They were fantastic. I didn't really mind playing anywhere. Once we started playing at football grounds like Burnden Park, Elland Road and Old Trafford that was a real eye opener from a player's point of view. They were tremendous places to play; the pitches were immaculate and so on. The dressing rooms for both teams would be decent. There were no rules for standards of dressing rooms in rugby league so as the away side, we would find ourselves getting changed in a room we couldn't swing a cat in. As players were putting our shorts on, they would bump into someone else.

My least favourite venue was probably the old Naughton Park which I thought was as rough as a bear's arse. It was a great place to play because they were a tenacious and tough team. The ground itself though wasn't so hot with tufts of grass all over the place.

One of the biggest tackles I had in my career was from a British player. He was a Wiganer who played for another Lancashire club. One time, we were playing them and I tried to go through this gap, he picked me up and near enough broke my neck. As I went over, my chin was in my chest. I always say to him when I see him, "You bastard". On a number of occasions in the 1980s I hurt my neck. That tackle stands out because my head concertinaed under my body. I thought I had put a hole in my chest with my chin. I carried on though, mindful that I wanted to play next week to pick up my pay. The physio did what he could. We played Hull KR and Millington, one of their props ran into me as I attempted a tackle, I hit his knee and damn near ripped my shoulder. It was giving me a lot of gyp and I couldn't sleep on my right hand side. I had treatment on it and continued playing with it. Every now and again though, I would take a hit on it and would get a shooting pain down the side of my neck. One day, I told the physio that the pain seemed to be extending down from my neck. He did some work on my upper arm and all of a sudden, it opened up. My bicep must have been torn off the bone. I lifted my A/C joint and played with that. It hurt like hell every time I hit it.

In the 1990s, while I was player-coaching the 'A' team then coaching the first team I would go into the gym to work out. I used to hit the bag and one day I hit it and my wrist bent over. I thought I had broken my wrist. I thought that maybe it needed strengthening so I got on the weights trying to strengthen it. It made no difference and got worse and worse until my right arm is the way it is today.

I now have a permanent injury to my right arm that has resulted in muscle wastage and loss of grip in my right hand. I went to a specialist and he told me that he thought I had some nerve damage. I had an operation and it was in a splint for a while. They took the splint off and it had made no difference. They did another major operation where they opened up my arm. They moved tendons and muscles into my right forearm so that I could hold my hand up. It's got worse though. Over the past five years or so, my tricep has gone and now my shoulder has started to waste. I've had to go back and see them and have more scans. I'm just wondering where will the wastage end? Is it going to go up to my neck? The specialist did tell me that they thought they had damaged my other nerve during one of the operations. I told him at least he was honest. I picked up a doctor in my cab recently to take him to Wrightington and he told me they had a machine now that they could use to stimulate and build the muscle. I didn't think they could do that without the nerve so I went back to see the specialist. He told me that that wasn't really the case and although it might do a bit, it wouldn't get it back to where it should be. He said we really needed to see what the cause of my problem is.

It's just part of the job. I have to get on with it. I can't lift what I used to do, I can't do what I used to do. I can't play tennis or darts because of my grip. I still do weight training, it's just that now one side's weaker than the other. I still row although my hands get pins and needles. I can run for about two miles before my arm starts dropping. I just have to make do.

I'm really proud of all my kids. Me eldest son, Vaughan, played as an amateur for St Judes; they got to the under–19s national cup final. They lost to Blackbrook, but they had Paul Wellens playing, they had a good side. St Judes had a strong side though with Mick Cassidy, Steve McCormack and Paul Norton. I enjoyed going to watch the games.

It was the same with my daughter Toni who used to play skittleball for the school. I would always go and watch her. Some of the kids would recognise me and be pointing me out. I'd have a great time with them.

Dwayne was the same, although early on he wouldn't play anything in terms of sport. I told him, "You're going to play something, I don't care if it's knucklebones or hopscotch, but you're going to play something, you're going to play a sport." A mate of mine came round and he had a son the same age as Dwayne, there was a vanload of them going to play rugby. My mate said, "Give us Dwayne's boots."

"You'll be bloody lucky," I replied. However, away he went. When he came home, that was it, he was playing from then on.

Initially, he was very timid on the tackling side, but he had a bit of ability when running with the ball. As time went on, he went to Deanery and Derek Birchall got hold of him. Unfortunately, I couldn't get to watch him in his first game. I saw him in the second game and was astounded, Dwayne was hitting them all over the place. It was bloody great to watch. Birchall had changed him a lot. There would be games where he would be up against a side full of good players a year older than him, but he would step through them and score a try.

Dwayne played in the under–15s at the same time that Terry Newton was playing under–16s alongside Paul Deacon. The under–15s played less games so they asked Dwayne to go straight through to the under–16s. I used to go and watch them play. I had a meeting with the club scouts and I asked them why they hadn't selected Terry Newton. They told me they felt they had that position covered. I said that he was a young Wiganer who was doing really well, but they didn't go for him. I thought the same with Deacon too. They both went to other clubs. There's always going to be some players that slip through the net. Terry was a very aggressive, good player. For some players, their quest for perfection can become overwhelming. They handle it in different ways. Sadly, in Terry's case, what's happened has happened.

Perhaps more talking and if players weren't treated as outcasts it would help them handle things.

Since I've come to this country I've seen players and people with big egos that have been larger than life characters and in some cases, very rough and physical characters. They've been a wee bit fragile in their personality and it's had devastating results. Perhaps talking more and being more in a team environment will help. It never helps a player if they're just left on the outside.

Dwayne signed for Wigan and was put in a real tough game to start with. His first team debut was against Saints, a massive game. He was unable to come up to the required standard that day. He had to step back and try again. If a player doesn't get the right guidance and a basic pattern for those big games, it becomes very difficult. The first thing is that he goes in nervous. He has to learn to try and control that, but it takes time and that's why it's called experience. If a player has ability then a basic pattern of play gives them something to work from. It means the team is structured and the forwards are doing their job. That's why I look back on Ces Mountford as a hell of a good coach because he put that structure in place and had confidence in his players.

Dwayne left Wigan to go to St Helens and was destined to play a part in arguably Saints' most famous try; the Chris Joynt last gasp play-off winner against Bradford in 2000. Thanks to Sky Sports' commentary, the try has become immortalised as "It's wide to West". We went to watch the game at Knowsley Road. Henry Paul was at Bradford at the time. My wife Maryann is Henry Paul's son Theo's godmother. We used to have Theo over when he was a little boy for two or three days at a time. It just so happened that we had Theo on the night of the game. We thought we would take him to watch his dad play against Saints. Dwayne was a sub for Saints that night. It got towards the end and Dwayne came on as a very late replacement. Paul Newlove had taken a heavy knock and was walking round in cloud cuckoo land. He wouldn't come off and Dwayne was desperate for him to get off. Dwayne pretty much hauled him off. The last tackle of the game started as the Bradford fans counted down to zero for the end of the game. Longy kicked it up then it just kept on and on. Suddenly, Dwayne was off down the touchline, pushing past Henry Paul on his way through, inside to Chris Joynt and that was it. We were all jumping up and down, yahooing and carrying on. Poor Theo was on the floor crying his eyes out wondering what was going on; we had forgotten about him.

We never used to go into the club after the game and Dwayne didn't much. He met us by the car as did Henry who greeted Dwayne with, "What's this pushing me off hey?" It was fantastic. That was the sort of thing Dwayne was capable of. However, his shoulder went at Saints. Sometimes, you come back too quickly; whether that's your own doing or the club doing it. It just didn't work. He went to Hull.

Dwayne went for a scan, the shoulder had come out three or four times. He was in agony and I was getting pissed off with it and wanted to know what was going on with the injury. The specialist said when it had come out, it had worn a bit of the cup. The Hull chairman said they would have to let him go. I think Dwayne got three months pay. That's the way rugby is sometimes.

I had wanted Dwayne to do an apprenticeship at 16, but he wouldn't do it because he wanted to be a rugby player. At 24, with his shoulder gone he came to me and told me he was going to do the apprenticeship. I was relieved, but warned him he would be on apprentice wages.

"That's alright," he said. "I can stay with you".

He did his apprenticeship even though one company went bust, he had to move to another place which he thought was not as good, but finally he ended up at the place he is now. People go through life and have to swap and change and it wasn't easy for him at times. He managed to get through it and now he's a qualified plumbing and heating engineer. He now has his own place with his partner Lisa and they're having a little boy at the beginning of September 2011.

Vaughan's got a little boy coming at the beginning of August 2011. That'll be his third child because he had one from a previous partner and already has one with his wife Joanne. Their names are Ellie Anne and Cameron.

My daughter Toni has a partner, Dan, he's been married before and has a little girl called Carmen. She's a little pearl. It's great having the grandkids round. The family is blossoming out quite well.

They've all moved out now so we're off back to New Zealand at the end of 2011. It's like when we brought the kids here to the UK and leaving the rest of the family at home, people have to make decisions in life. I get so many people in my taxi who say: "Oh, I could never leave my mum."

I ask them, "What about your life?"

"My life's around my mum."

"What if something happens to your mum? That's something you don't want to see, but age will tell that for us all. We don't live forever. When that happens you think 'I wish I'd done this or I wish I'd done that'."

When you're away from them, you love talking to them, but you're not on their doorstep all the time. When they do pass on, you miss them, of course, but you're not totally devastated by it. You always remember the good times. I used to go back to New Zealand and have great times with my dad up until his death six years ago. We'd go out for meals and I'd take him to the races. I did used to say to him though, "If something happens, I won't be coming back." I would always go and see him when I went over, would always keep in touch on the phone, but if something happened to him, I wouldn't be going over. I told him I wouldn't expect him to come to the UK if something sudden happened to me either. We'd have enjoyed our time together. One of my sons says, "Don't talk about that."

"Listen," I reply. "These are things that happen in life. This is why I brought you to the UK, to see the world. I've had the opportunity to show you kids the world. We've had great times together so if anything happens to you, it would kill me, but I'll know I couldn't have done anything else for you. If something happens to me, you know the old chap's done alright. I've had a great time so don't worry about me, get on with your life." These are things you don't want to think about, but it happens.

We are looking forward to going home. The winters in England are harsh and as you get older, you want a bit more sun on your back. We had thought about it for a while. It's like coming here in the first place; it's a challenge. We'll miss the kids and the grandkids but they need time to blossom on their own as well. We can come across and if they need help, we can help them. Also, they need to come across to New Zealand and have a look. It might be that some of them stay there.

I don't want to get back involved with rugby league when I go back to New Zealand. I've had enough. We stay with one of my mates, Bud Lisle when we go back to New Zealand and we have a marvellous time.

We have a house there and he and his partner look after it for us. They've done a great job for us. Bud was instrumental in helping me throughout my career as well. He goes to the RSA (Returned and Services Association) and he must have mentioned to someone that I was coming back. Someone told Bud that they had a job for me. It's a franchise minibus company doing runs from the airport at night. I looked into it and it sounds alright. When I go back, I am going to sit the test for the licence then go and do it. It's the type of thing I want to do. I don't want to go back and be involved as director of coaching anywhere. I'm not saying that in a detrimental way, but I've done my 40 years. Forty years and you get a pension!

I like the area we live in. We ended up moving to a detached house on the border between Marus Bridge and Winstanley. It's been fantastic and we've had marvellous neighbours. At one point, my wife wanted us to buy another house, but I told her I was very happy where I was. If I want to walk to town, I can do.

As for rugby league, when four substitutes and 12 replacements came into the game, it was really good for the coach. The coach could bring a player off who was out of control.

"Why are you bringing me off?"

"Because you were acting the way you are now, out of control. Sit down and shut up and I'll put you back on in a bit."

Given time to quieten down they'd tell you, "I'm sorry about that, you're right."

If he had kicked off and smacked someone, he could have been sitting on the bench for the rest of the game. It's been great for the game because not only can the coach change players around to enable the team to play at a higher level, but he can also diffuse certain situations.

The rule change I wanted to be implemented when I was still playing was to have the scrum the way it is now. They used to have to put three scrums down to get one ball out. Hookers had their feet out of the scrum, it was a total balls up. The scrums were that tight my ears used to bleed, I got pissed off with it.

The other change I would have introduced was the move to summer rugby. I didn't want to be playing in the winter freezing my bollocks off. Soon after I finished playing, they switched to summer rugby.

There are some retired hookers who say, "The hooking role has gone out of the game." That's a load of rubbish because the hooker is more important now than ever. He directs things from dummy half, passes the ball and runs with it.

In terms of the game today, I just wish the England team would step up to the plate. I think that overall there are too many overseas players in Britain. They make all the noises about developing the game, but they are not doing it the way they should. The players aren't coming through, less milk, less cream.

Hawera as a town had about eight primary schools that all fed into an intermediate school then there was the high school. When I was in primary school, Friday afternoon was sports afternoon. We'd all jump on our bikes and head to the rugby area. We'd all play each other. At the end of the year there was a tournament between all the teams with a cup presented to the winner. Additionally, all the primary schools would have their own athletics meeting. The winners from each school would go forward to a 'champion of champions' tournament. I was pretty good at athletics so was champion of my school and went on to become champion of champions. I wasn't so good at swimming; I'd give it a shot though. They did exactly the same thing with swimming with all the schools. It was really good and all the teachers were really interested in sport. It was a big thing. I've championed all that in Britain. I cannot understand why that sort of thing cannot be done here.

I coached at a Wigan primary school for three and a half years, in that time, we had one competitive game. That was against Worsley Mesnes. There were girls playing for our side and they loved it. One of them was pushing the boys off left, right and centre. I don't know what the problem was with the teachers. I don't know whether they were worried the kids would get injured and there would be claims against them or whether they didn't have the time. There was a tag rugby tournament where one player would take another's tag off to stop them, that was good because it taught them skills. The lack of competitive sport though was damaging. The part that disappointed me most was I would get the kids for coaching for an hour on a Monday afternoon. As it was touch rugby, we would concentrate on moving the ball around and having games where they could enjoy themselves. Then I'd do about 10 minutes where they could tackle, but it would be

124

done at walking pace. I'd teach them how to tackle from the side and from the back, all the techniques like keeping their head to one side so they wouldn't get hurt. They got pretty good at it. The problem was I'd get calls from the teacher saying: "It's too cold today" or "It's too hot today" or "It's raining today" and the kids wouldn't be allowed to train. I would be standing there, waiting around. It was like being a nail being hit by a hammer, just keeping getting knocked down and down. I was coaching at St Judes at the time and one of the other coaches told me he was coaching a school down the road from my school. I said that it was bloody hard work getting games and he said he had the same problem. We decided we would get a game together between the two schools which were only 200 metres apart. We couldn't do it. It was bloody ridiculous.

Over the summer holidays, I was told the kids would be taken to Robin Park one day for about half past one. I told them I would meet them there. I got there about twenty five past and they arrived at about twenty five to. The first thing the teacher said was, "It's very cold on these children's legs" and they were going to play inside! At about five to two, the teacher said, "We have to take them back to school now." What was the point? I waited until the next holiday and I just didn't go back. I just thought, "What an absolute waste of time." It wasn't worth me putting my time and effort in because half the time I wasn't wanted.

What I believe is that sport teaches kids a lot of good values of life. Sport taught me such things as learning to win and lose, responsibility to the coach and fellow players, timekeeping, learning a skill, keeping fit, being healthy and disciplined. Looking at the makeup of an average classroom in Britain, there might be 25 young people in that classroom. There will be 15 who are interested, their parents are interested and everything's great. There might be five who are there or thereabouts, the parents might come down but they're not so bothered. Then there are five where the parents couldn't care less. Lose those kids and they end up on street corners. If the class get into sport, then definitely the five who are sort of interested will be involved and also maybe three of the kids who weren't. Get them into sport and it will stop them causing trouble. The coach will keep in touch with them and the parents of the kids who are really interested will take those other kids under their wing. They learn good things off these role models that they aren't getting at home. It would take a lot of kids out of bad situations in Britain, that's what happens in New Zealand and Australia. One or two will always be missed, but look at the gangs like 'The Black Power' and 'The Mongrel Mob', they're playing sport. They get on that park and if they're playing each other, they knock the stuffing out of each other. They get good crowds because they are so into it. They learn the rules though and if the ref blows his whistle and says, "That's enough, you're off" they walk.

It's a big thing with me. At the moment, the education system focuses on the academic side. Companies who have billions and billions of pounds are seeking young people for all types of jobs in industry. What schools don't seem to do is cater for young people who aren't academically minded but are more gifted at sport. What people should realise is that every sport now has vast amounts of money. By having sport in schools they could channel these young people into those areas, for example, playing players at fully professional, semi-professional and amateur level. There are also opportunities for physios, administrators, grounds staff, right down to stewards on match day. There are thousands of opportunities that I don't think people are being pushed towards, all the way through from association football to wrestling.

I just think that if the government said they wanted competitive sports in schools they could ask people on Jobseeker's Allowance at interviews if they had previously played sport. If they were interested in coaching, they would be given another £50 a week on top of their dole money. They would then be sent into a school for two years to coach once or twice a week. They could do the same to get more referees involved in sport. They could offer similar incentives to people who have retired. Teachers could concentrate on academic matters and these people could be invaluable instead of left in limbo on the streets.

The government would also have to bring in legislation that eases off this claiming culture of health and safety gone mad. I just think if something happened to my kids if they got hurt after the teachers left them unsupervised, I'd go down and kick up 'bobsy die'. However, if my kid gets hurt playing sport or gets their arse kicked for not doing something I would support the teachers.

People say Britain can't compete at rugby league, but I think it's a bigger problem than that; it's the whole sporting structure in this country. In America, New Zealand or Australia, they compete at every sport. That comes from being sports orientated and starts within the schools. There are enough people here to get it going. Look at it this way; I'm not so sure how far rugby league is going to go forward in Britain. When I first came over to this country, it was in the schools and there were the amateur clubs. Some of the kids were overplayed by playing for their school and their amateur club.

When I first came over here, another Kiwi who had played for North Sydney and gone to Leeds and I were asked to go to the Rugby Football League and talk about the game. They wanted to know why New Zealand and Australia were better prepared than Britain and what were they doing that was different. I told them that in each of those countries, there was just one organisation running the game. There were two or three organisations running the game over here. I said they would be better trying to get them under the one roof. I think now, as I did then, that the best way of running rugby league would be putting it in the schools. If the training sessions are enjoyable, such as 'touch rugby', then the kids want to come and play. At school level, they could teach them 'touch rugby' and all the finer arts of the game. They could still be taught to tackle as well, but go through it slowly and get everything right with it. At primary school, with kids learning 'touch rugby' they could learn how to pass the ball, how to kick, how to step and so on. At secondary school level, then bring in the tackling. At 16, the professional clubs should take the best ones and the amateur teams should take the rest.

When I first came to Wigan, I bet there were about 20 to 30 schools playing rugby league at each age level. Now there's probably only five or six amateur clubs in Wigan playing rugby at different age groups and they do a really good job. When there are more people coming into the game, there are more good ones coming out on top. It needs looking at. Another important issue is obviously people being cleared to be able to coach kids in terms of child protection. If it all worked, there would be more English players playing for the top teams. There would also be less people on the dole because kids who previously would have been lost would have got a bit more of a start in life. They'd be trying to find jobs instead of trying to find trouble.

If someone played rugby as a kid, where are their mates? They are the fellows they played alongside. They are the fellows they've made friends with through working. They all help each other. One of them may be out of work and they know someone who might have a job for them and so on. One of their mates may help them with the plumbing and he can do something for them. If one of them is down, all the rest gather round and have a chat and a beer with him. It's a support network that they have with their friends. It makes for a better community.

In terms of England competing at the highest level, just watch a State of Origin game then watch the Exiles match. The Exiles team had one current international, the rest had either not made it or are finished. Even so, England lost.

I honestly can't see the England team changing much. It's all very well having a game against the Exiles and a few extra training sessions, but what's that going to do. Phil Clarke summed it up in a nutshell before the Exiles game had been played. He said that New Zealand and Australia have specialist players in key positions. Now and again, there might be an exception where a loose-forward plays stand-off for Australia such as Lewis or Fittler, but they were exceptions. Phil went through the England line up and said there is Sam Tomkins at full-back, but he's played a lot of rugby at half-back. There was Luke Robinson at hooker, but he's played a lot of rugby at half-back. Then the stand-off, Kevin Sinfield, plays the majority of the time at loose-forward. They're all over the place. Why can't they go out and pick the best in each position? Don't select players because you think they'll do a good job, put them in because they are the best in that position. Then they will see they don't have the specialists.

Look at the Wigan team in the 1980s and 1990s, they provided most of the players for the Great Britain side. The coaching was right, the development was right and the schools and amateurs were firing. As a result of this, Great Britain were competing against Australia and would beat them now and again. Once Wigan were no longer top dogs, I believe that the RFL wanted to bring Wigan back with the mob. What they should have done was try and get everybody else up to Wigan's level. I just despair for the game to be honest, it might go backwards if it hasn't already. Super League is good and a great platform for the game, but we need to get the young English players up to that standard. Wigan have started doing it, but it needs to be done more.

From a New Zealand point of view, it's great to see that they won the World Cup and Four Nations. They have had a hell of a change in getting there. A few years ago, they had some people in charge who I thought just wanted to go on tours and weren't so concerned with the development of the game. There were a lot of problems. The New Zealand Rugby League had bought pubs with slot machines in and there was a bit of hanky panky going on. They were told two or three years ago that if they didn't get their act together there would be a judicial review of the whole setup and they would lose their government funding called 'Spark'. A judge went in and carried out a full review, they got rid of the board of directors. They more or less turned everything over and got a new board of directors in. A new development process was put in place and it's really started to pay off. There's still a bit to do, but it's a hell of a lot better than it was. I get their newsletters and there's lots going on, they have directors in each area and more kids playing the game. They have people like Ruben Wiki going round doing coaching courses and so on. They still won the Tri Nations under the old way of doing things, but now the situation should get better. They've got a New Zealand wide competition, they've got the Warriors playing in the NRL as well as scouts throughout New Zealand looking for players to go and play for other teams in the NRL to gain experience.

With Maryann and the children at home in Wigan.

The newspapers wanted a photo of Graeme's big feet when he arrived in Wigan.

Coaching youngsters in Wigan was always enjoyable.
(Both photos courtesy *Wigan Observer*)

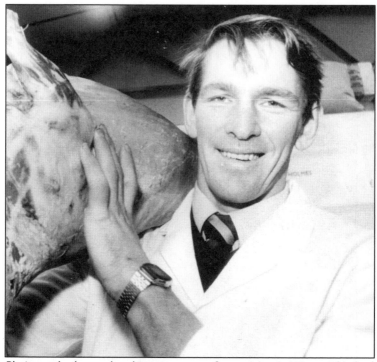

Photographed as a slaughterman soon after arriving in Wigan. This had been Graeme's job in New Zealand, but he never did the job in Wigan.

Ready for a passenger – as a taxi driver in Wigan.
(Peter Lush)

13. Reflections

The Haka is a fantastic thing to get Kiwis going and helps us remember that we're a New Zealanders. Look at the meaning of it and it goes back to when they used to go on the ridges when a village was under attack and do the Haka. They'd then run down and give it to them. You see Isaac Luke doing it today with his eyes rolling in the back of his head, it's a real pick-me-up. It's their heritage. New Zealand now is getting more into trying to keep the Maori heritage. They want to keep it alive so it doesn't die and trying to reintroduce the Maori language. It's a good thing. The Maori are the original New Zealanders. It's like the Aborigines, it's good to see any indigenous people keep their heritage. I think it's something that needs to be learnt in the UK. Yes, you want to see people fit into your way of life and society, but you also want to see them have their own identity. I went to school with Chinese kids and Indian kids. Their mums would wear saris and I used to think it was marvellous. We would go round each other's houses on our birthdays. They all kept their identity, but were all New Zealanders. It would be nice to see that in England where people would all fit together, but there would be tolerance. Hopefully in the future it will happen. I see at the moment in the taxis people making negative comments about Pakistanis for example. I say, "Hey, how did they get here in the first place? Your granddad brought them in to work here". I then tell them that they have been in the country longer than you, and they need to chill out.

My accent creates a lot of interest, I get confused for being South African or Australian – the latter followed by "Oh we shouldn't have called a Kiwi that" when I've told them where I come from. One fellow got out of the cab once and said, "Now then owd chap, what do I owe thee?"

"Less of the old chap," I replied.

The idea of driving a taxi came to me in 1977 when I went to watch the Australian Grand Final between St George and Parramatta. When we got there, we were picked up by a taxi that was owned by Roy Masters, one of the coaches in Sydney. We were talking and he told me he had it easy as he just worked when he wanted to. I thought, "That sounds alright". At the end of my career, I thought about what I wanted to do. I didn't want to sit on my arse all day and I didn't want to have to do a nine-to-five job somewhere with a boss moaning like hell if I wanted some time off. I thought I would try taxi driving. I had a mate with a black cab called John Brogan. I rang him to say I fancied giving it a go and could I use his cab once a week? He said that would be fine. I tried it and realised it would suit me. I then bought my own taxi. I've had it for 11 years now. At first, it could be tricky when people were asking me to take them to places which I wasn't sure how to get to. Most people would help me out and if I ever got really stuck, I would consult my map. It was good having decent banter with most people too.

Not long after I started, I took a fellow to the fair they used to have on the car park behind Hindley town centre. He got in and abruptly said, "Take me to Hindley town centre." We got there and he said, "You can get stuffed, I'm not paying you." I said, "Oh yeah?" He got out and started walking down the road. I thought that we would see about that. I parked the car up, he went round one way and I went round the other. I saw him, crept up behind him and grabbed him. I asked him, "Who's not paying?" The wrestling training helped me because I bent his nose as he continued to tell me he wasn't going to pay me. He finally told me he would pay as his nose started bleeding. He passed me a tenner with blood all over it. I told him, "Fair enough, don't do it again." As I drove away, he came out and threw a rubbish bin at my cab which missed by miles. When I took my takings into John and he saw the bloody £10 note, he asked what had happened and I just told him he would have to ask the man at the fair about that. That sort of things happens very rarely though. I use a simple strategy, if they look a bit dicey I ask them for money upfront.

Once I went to Bolton and the young guy in the back told me he would just nip out to get his money. Off he went down the road and Martin Offiah wouldn't have beaten him. If I'd have caught him, I'd have signed him up. He had set off like a streak of weasel piss.

One man I have to mention is the fellow who used to do work on my taxi for me. His name was Brian Pollitt. The first time I walked into his garage, this little guy came walking towards me saying, "Don't think you can come round here pushing in because you played for Wigan rugby." I just said, "Who cut your hair?" I got on with him straight away. He was a real little character. He fixed my car from that day on. Even if my car didn't need fixing, I would go down and have a laugh with him. Unfortunately, he died a couple of years ago. His son Darren fixes my car now.

There's some characters on the rank itself, we had this fellow called 'Wurzel' although David was his real name. He was a big bloke and would sit in his cab in the queue at the train station. What would happen is if a driver was at the front of the queue, they would pick up a fare and everybody would move up. However, Wurzel would sit in his cab and fall asleep. We had to beep to wake him up which we ended up getting sick of doing. One night, he fell asleep there and they all left him. They just nipped their cabs round his while he slept. Everybody went home shortly after the last train came in around midnight. Apparently, he woke up around half past one and finally left the car park.

There are drivers who bullshit a lot and try and tell me how much they made last night. I look at them and think they could have gone to London and back and they wouldn't have made that much. Then there are those who complain it's a hard night and I think it can't be as bad as they're making out. There are all types of characters there. I can have a good craic with some of them and get to hear all the new jokes.

The people I pick up are great. I have been asked loads of times for autographs or to get out to have my photograph taken with them. The majority of people are fine.

I enjoy doing it out of sight. It suits my lifestyle because I can go out to work when I want. I usually go out about seven and come home about midnight during the week. I then do nine till about four on a Friday and Saturday. I have all the days to myself. It doesn't make me a fortune, but it suits me.

It's amazing how many people get in and say "You should be doing this" or "You should be doing that," they say I should be commentating or coaching. Then there are others who think I have fallen on hard times. I just ask them what hours they work and when they say nine-to-five, I just tell them, "I work when I feel like it." If I want to go to New Zealand I park my cab up then when I come back six to eight weeks later I jump back in and go to work. There's no boss telling me what to do.

Some get in and want to reminisce about games from years ago, they say, "I suppose everybody asks you this..." but I tell them it's ok. There are lots of memories. Some get in and tell me they were at

Leeds when I played my first game for Wigan. It was pissing it down when I got to Leeds, it was cold and there was sleet and snow shooting down. I remember thinking, "What have I come to here?" I got changed after the game and couldn't find where the players were having something to eat. I asked some supporters and they helped me out, I had a chat to them.

When I came to England, it was two weeks before my 29th birthday and I'm going to be 58 in December 2011. I've been over here half my life. I came over quite late for a player. When they asked me how old I was, I replied, "27". I had to keep remembering to say I was born in 55 but if I ever needed to put it down officially it was 53. They found out after a while. I played first team until I was 36. I then player-coached the 'A' team until I was 42. In that time I played a couple of first team games when needed. I then played in the union leg of the cross code challenge against Bath at 43.

My son Vaughan played in the Ken Gee tournament for workshop sides. He asked me if I fancied a game and I said "Yeah, I do". They were allowed two pros so Dave Wood, a bloke who had played for Wigan in the early days and I turned out for them. I played two years in a row. People said to me that I would take some serious stick playing against amateurs. I asked them what they meant and they said they would all be into me. I just asked: "What do you think the pros do?" Amateurs aren't going to do any more damage than the pros did to me. I played for the under–19s at 40 and St Pats' first team only just beat us. I always wanted to play but when it came time to step back, it was no problem. It's like now where I have no involvement with the game; it's not a problem. I'd had enough of playing.

I played at amateur level, 'A' team, first team and international, I've coached kids, 'A' team, first team, Super League, First Division, Second Division and amateur level. I've done it all.

I'd like to be remembered as a player who gave it my best shot. I enjoyed the game out of sight and got a lot out of the game. I worked for it though. Sometimes it worked for me, sometimes it didn't. I loved playing it. If you're going to do it, go out and give it your best shot. You can still have fun, but do that extra bit of work to make you play to your potential.

I decided to write this book to explain the enjoyment I had in Wigan, it's not just about rugby, it's things that have happened around

Wigan, including my days on the taxis and in the gym. Another reason is that a mate in New Zealand said I should write a book because people will want to know what's gone on and happened in your life. The main reason though, and what my wife has said, is that the book will be for our future family. They want to know who the old fellow was. If they find out that their Great Granddad or their Great-great Granddad played for Wigan they will read the book and learn all about it. "That was the old fellow." When they see Maryann's name they will say "That was my Grandma" or "That was my Great Grandma."

Our time in Great Britain has been marvellous, the playing time has been great, the camaraderie playing together was fantastic too. I was really privileged to be able to sign to come here. That was mainly because of Ces Mountford and his crew who recommended I come here and helped organise it. I've had a marvellous time and even though I'm going back to New Zealand, I'll be coming back to visit.

I went through some times where I was put down a bit, but for me, that was part of learning that I had to step up again. I didn't take anyone telling me that I couldn't do something. I had to be able to prove them wrong. The people I might have criticised in this book, in the end I have to thank them because they showed me some of the wrong ways to do things. It made me think that if I had a chance, I could do it a better way. Everybody makes mistakes, during my career I made one or two, but in the end, overall I think I was really satisfied. I enjoyed it out of sight. I did what I wanted to do and if I had to live my life again, I'd do it again.

My boss at the pools office, Billy Blan, was a real stickler on bad language and I would have had to apologise to him for using a couple in the book. I found as a coach that I could be as quiet, restrained and technical as I wanted, but every now and again I had to get up and do my thing! The results were amazing.

I'd like to thank the following people for their help; my family without whom I would never have kept the interest up, they have been with me all the time, Ces Mountford and family, Bud Lisle and his partner Janet Lebout who have really helped us out with what we've been doing in New Zealand, the supporters throughout rugby league; they made it all possible, from Hawera right to the top of Cumbria.

Appendix: Statistics and records

(The research for the New Zealand statistics was done by Robert Gate, otherwise by Peter Lush. Some of the records for matches in New Zealand are not complete.)

International playing career for New Zealand

18 tests between 1975 and 1985 (Kiwi number 517)
2 tries in test matches
36 matches including the test matches, 8 tries and 1 goal

1975:	Australia (World Champ)	A	Lost 8-36
1979:	Great Britain	H	Lost 8-16 (Captain)
	Great Britain	H	Lost 7-22 (Captain)
1980:	Australia	H	Lost 6-27 (Sub)
	Australia	H	Lost 6-15 (Sub)
	Great Britain	A	Drew 14-14
	Great Britain	A	Won 12-8
	Great Britain	A	Lost 2-10
	France	A	Lost 5-6
	France	A	Won 11-3
1981:	France	H	Won 26-3
	France	H	Won 25-2
1982:	Australia	A	Lost 8-11
	Australia	A	Lost 2-20
	Papua New Guinea	A	Won 56-5 1 try
1983:	Australia	H	Lost 4-16 (Sub)
	Australia	A	Won 19-12 (Captain) 1 try
1985:	Great Britain	A	Lost 8-25

Won: 6 Drawn: 1 Lost: 11

Played against:
Australia 7 times   France 4 times
Great Britain 6 times   Papua New Guinea once

Tour matches (including tests)

	App	Sub	Tries	Points
Australia 1975	3	0	3	9
Great Britain 1980	9	0	2	6
France 1980	4	0	0	0
Australia & PNG 1982	11	0	2	8 (includes 1 goal)

New Zealand playing career

Stratford:
1971:   Won the Price Cup Breweries Trophy and Champion of Champions

Hawera:
1972:   Player of the Year. Runners-up in senior championship

Taranaki:
1971:   I try (At least 1 appearance)
1972:   4 tries (At least 3 appearances). Nominated for Rothmans Special Coaching Programme
1973 & 1974:   Not known
1975:   7 appearances, 5 tries. One of 5 players of the Year for Taranaki
1976:   1 try (At least 3 appearances). Captained Taranaki's National Seven-a-side winning team at Wellington. Scored 2 tries in final. Taranaki's first national title win.
1977:   4 tries (At least 4 appearances). Taranaki captain.
1978:   8 tries, appearances not known. Captain of Taranaki who "repulsed six challenges for the NZRL Cup and regained the National Sevens trophy in its most successful season ever" (NZRL Annual)
1979:   8 tries, including 4 in a match against Manawatu, appearances not known. First Taranaki player to captain New Zealand.
1980 & 1981: Not known.
1982:   5 tries, appearances not known.
1983:   6 tries, 2 appearances. Scored six tries in one match against Wellington

Central Districts:
1979:   2 tries, 3 appearances. Central Districts won National Districts Competition.
1980 & 1981: Not known.
1982:   2 tries, 3 appearances. Central Districts won National Districts Competition.

North Island:
1973:   Played against South Island at Wellington, lost 16-12
1974:   Played against Auckland and Great Britain
1975:   Played against England
1976:   Played against Sydney

New Zealand trial matches:
1977:   2 appearances, for New Zealand XIII against Southern Zone, and for Northern Zone against New Zealand XIII (as sub).

Awards:
Joint Sportsman of the Year in 1978 (with Graham Waite)
Joint New Zealand Player of the Year in 1978 (1979 NZRL Annual)
Joint New Zealand Player of the Year in 1983 (1983 NZRL Annual)
2008: Included in Taranaki Team of the Century

Wigan playing career

Season	App	Sub	Tries	Points
1982–83	21	0	7	21
1983–84	36	0	13	52
1984–85	38	1	8	32
1985–86	31	5	10	40
1986–87	28	5	6	24
1987–88	28	6	4	16
1989–90	1	0	0	0
1990–91	2	0	1	4
Totals:	**185**	**17**	**49**	**189**

Honours:

Stones Bitter Championship (First Division):
Winners 1986–87 Pl: 30 W: 28 D: 0 L: 2 Pts: 56 F: 941 A: 193

Challenge Cup:
Winners: 1984–85; Runners–up: 1983–84

John Player Trophy / John Player Special Trophy:
Winners: 1982–83, 1985–86, 1986–87

Premiership:
Winners: 1986–87

Lancashire Cup:
Winners: 1986–87, 1987–88; Runners–up: 1984–85

World Club Challenge:
Winners: 1987–88

Charity Shield:
Winners: 1985–86, 1987–88

Finals:

Challenge Cup:
1983–84: Wigan 6 Widnes 19
Wigan: S. Edwards, D. Ramsdale, D. Stephenson, C. Whitfield, H. Gill,
M. Cannon, G. Stephens, K. Hemsley, H. Tamati, B. Case, G. West (capt.), M.
Scott, J. Pendlebury. Subs: W. Elvin, B. Juliff.
Scorers: Try: Hemsley; Goal: Whitfield
Widnes: M. Burke, S. Wright, E. Hughes, J. Lydon, J. Basnett, K. O'Loughlin,
A. Gregory, S. O'Neill, K. Elwell, K. Tamati, L. Gorley, M. O'Neill, M. Adams.
Subs: D. Hulme, F. Whitfield.
Scorers: Tries: Lydon 2, O'Loughlin; Goals: Burke 3; Drop–goal: O'Neill.

1984–85: Wigan 28 Hull 24
Wigan: S. Edwards, J. Ferguson, D. Stephenson, S. Donlan, H. Gill, B. Kenny, M. Ford, N. Courtney, N. Kiss, B. Case, G. West (capt.), B. Dunn, I. Potter. Subs: N. Du Toit (dnp), D. Campbell.
Scorers: Tries: Ferguson 2, Kenny, Gill, Edwards; Goals: Gill 3, Stephenson.
Hull: G. Kemble, K. James, S. Evans, J. Leuluai, D. O'Hara, F. Ah Kuoi, P. Sterling, L. Crooks, S. Patrick, N. Puckering, J. Muggleton, P. Rose, S. Norton. Subs: G. Schofield, G. Divorty.
Scorers: Tries: Leuluai 2, James, Evans, Divorty; Goals: Crooks 2.

John Player Trophy / John Player Special Trophy:
1982–83: Wigan 15 Leeds 4
Wigan: B. Williams, D. Ramsdale, D. Stephenson, C. Whitfield, H. Gill, M. Foy, J. Fairhurst, G. Shaw, N. Kiss, D. Campbell, G. West, M. Scott, J. Pendlebury. Subs: B. Case, B. Juliff.
Scorers: Tries: Gill, Juliff; Goals: Whitfield 4; Drop–goals: Whitfield.
Leeds: N. Hague, M. Campbell, I. Wilkinson, L. Dyl, A. Smith, J. Holmes, Kevin Dick, R. Dickinson, D. Ward, T. Burke, A. Sykes, W. Heron, D. Heron.
Scorer: Goals: Dick 2.

1985–86: Wigan 11 Hull KR 8
Wigan: S. Hampson, R. Mordt, D. Stephenson, E. Hanley, H. Gill, S. Ella, M. Ford, G. Dowling, N. Kiss, S. Wane, G. West (capt.), A. Goodway, I. Potter. Subs: S. Edwards, N. Du Toit.
Scorers: Tries: Wane, Ford; Goal: Stephenson; Drop–goal: Dowling.
Hull KR: J. Lydiat, G. Clark, M. Smith, J. Dorahy, D. Laws, G. Smith, P. Harkin, P. Johnston, D. Watkinson, A. Ema, C. Burton, A. Kelly, G. Miller. Subs: I. Robinson, C. Rudd (dnp).
Scorers: Tries: Lydiat, Laws.

1986–87: Wigan 18 Warrington 4
Wigan: S. Hampson, D. Stephenson, J. Lydon, D. Bell, H. Gill, E. Hanley, S. Edwards, G. West (capt.), M. Dermott, B. Case, I. Roberts, I. Potter, A. Goodway. Subs: M. Ford, R. Louw.
Scorers: Tries: Gill 2, Goodway, Bell; Goal: Gill.
Warrington: B. Johnson, K. Meadows, P. Cullen, J. Ropati, M. Forster, K. Kelly, S. Peters, L. Boyd, K. Tamati, B. Jackson, G. Sanderson, M. Roberts, M. Gregory. Subs: R. Duane, A. Rathbone.
Scorer: Try: Forster.

Premiership:
1986–87: Wigan 8 Warrington 0
Wigan: S. Hampson, H. Gill, D. Stephenson, D. Bell, J. Lydon, S. Edwards, A. Gregory, B. Case, N. Kiss, S. Wane, A. Goodway, I. Potter, E. Hanley. Subs: R. Russell, G. West.
Scorers: Try: Lydon; Goals: Stephenson, Gill.
Warrington: B. Johnson, D. Drummond, J. Ropati, B. Peters, M. Forster, P. Cullen, P. Bishop, K. Tamati, M. Roberts, B. Jackson, T. Humphries, G. Sanderson, R. Duane. Subs: M. Gregory, B. Eccles.

Lancashire Cup:

1984–85: Wigan 18 St Helens 26
Wigan: S. Edwards, J. Ferguson, D. Stephenson, C. Whitfield, H. Gill, M. Cannon, J. Fairhurst. N. Courtney, N. Kiss, B. Case, G. West (capt.), S. Wane, I. Potter. Subs: J. Pendlebury, M. Scott (dnp).
Scorers: Tries: Gill, West, Kiss; Goals: Whitfield 3.
St Helens: P. Veivers, B. Ledger, S. Allen, M. Meninga, S. Day, C. Arkwright, N. Holding, T. Burke, G. Liptrot, P. Gorley, A. Platt, P. Round, H. Pinner. Subs: J. Smith (dnp), R. Haggerty.
Scorers: Tries: Meninga 2, Haggerty, Day; Goals: Day 5.

1986–87: Wigan 27 Oldham 6
Wigan: S. Edwards, J. Lydon, D. Stephenson, D. Bell, H. Gill, E. Hanley, M. Ford, G. West (capt.), M. Dermott, B. Case, I. Roberts, I. Potter, A. Goodway. Subs: S. Hampson, R. Louw.
Scorers: Tries: Edwards 2, Ford, Lydon; Goals: Gill 5; Drop–goal: Lydon.
Oldham: H. M'Barki, P. Sherman, G. Bridge, G. Warnecke, M. Taylor, D. Topliss, P. Kirwan, B. Clark, T. Flanagan, D. Hobbs, T. Nadiole, M. Worrall, S. Raper. Subs: N. Clawson (dnp), C. Hawkyard.
Scorers: Try: Bridge; Goal: Hobbs.

1987–88: Wigan 28 Warrington 16
Wigan: S. Hampson, R. Russell, D. Stephenson, J. Lydon, H. Gill, S. Edwards, A. Gregory, B. Case, N. Kiss, S. Wane, A. Goodway, I. Potter, E. Hanley. Subs: D. Bell, G. West.
Scorers: Tries: Hanley 2, Gill, West; Goals: Lydon 5, Stephenson.
Warrington: B. Johnson, D. Drummond, M. Forster, B. Peters, B. Carbert, J. Woods, K. Holden, K. Tamati, C. Webb, T. Humphries, G. Sanderson, M. Roberts, M. Gregory. Subs: D. Lyon (dnp), N. Harmon.
Scorers: Tries: Forster 2, Gregory; Goals: Woods 2.

World Club Challenge:

1987–88: Wigan 8 Manly–Warringah 2
Wigan: S. Hampson, R. Russell, D. Stephenson, J. Lydon, H. Gill, S. Edwards, A. Gregory, B. Case, N. Kiss, S. Wane, A. Goodway, I. Potter, E. Hanley. Subs: G. Byrne (dnp), G. West (dnp), I. Gildart (dnp), I. Lucas.
Scorer: Goals: Stephenson 4.
Manly–Warringah: D. Shearer, D. Ronson, D. Williams, M. O'Connor, S. Davis, C. Lyons, D. Hasler, P. Daley, M. Cochrane, I. Gately, R. Gibbs, O. Cunningham, P. Vautin. Subs: M. Brokenshire, J. Ticehurst, M. Pocock (dnp), P. Shaw.
Scorer: Goal: O' Connor.

Charity Shield:

1985–86: Wigan 34 Hull KR 6
Wigan: S. Hampson, P. Ford, D. Stephenson, S. Donlan, H. Gill, S. Edwards, M. Ford, N. Courtney, N. Kiss, D. Campbell, G. West, N. Du Toit, S. Wane. Subs: I. Lucas, J. Mayo.
Scorers: Tries: Donlan 2, Gill 2, M. Ford; Goals: Stephenson 7.

Hull KR: G. Fairbairn, G. Clark, I. Robinson, G. Prohm, D. Laws, M. Smith, G. Smith, D. Harrison, D. Watkinson, A. Ema, A. Kelly, C. Burton, P. Hogan. Subs: C. Rudd, J. Lydiat.
Scorers: Try: Clark; Goal: Lydiat.

1987–88: Wigan 44 Halifax 12
Wigan: S. Hampson, D. Stephenson, G. Byrne, D. Bell, H. Gill, S. Edwards, A. Gregory, G. West (capt.), N. Kiss, B. Case, I. Gildart, I. Potter, A. Goodway. Subs: R. Russell, S. Wane.
Scorers: Tries: Edwards 2, Bell 2, Hampson 2, Gill; Goals: Stephenson 8.
Halifax: G. Eadie, M. Taylor, S. Wilson, T. Anderson, W. George, A. Simpson, G. Stephens, R. Dickinson, J. Pendlebury, G. Beevers, N. James, M. Scott, P. Dixon. Subs: B. Juliff, P. Bell.
Scorers: Tries: Dixon, Juliff; Goals: Eadie 2.

Wigan coaching career

Honours:

World Club Challenge:
Winners 1993–94 Wigan 20 Brisbane Broncos 14

Stones Bitter Championship:
Winners 1994–95 Pl: 30 W: 28 D: 0 L: 2 Pts: 56 F: 1148 A: 386

Centenary Championship:
Winners 1995–96 Pl: 20 W: 18 D: 0 L: 2 Pts: 36 F: 810 A: 316

Challenge Cup:
Winners: 1994–95 Wigan 30 Leeds 10

Regal Trophy:
Winners:
1994–95: Wigan 40 Warrington 10; 1995–96: Wigan 25 St Helens 16

Premiership:
Winners:
1993–94: Wigan 24 Castleford 20; 1994–95: Wigan 69 Leeds 12

Charity Shield:
Winners: 1995–96 Wigan 45 Leeds 20

Middlesex Sevens (Rugby union):
Winners: 1996

Summary:
Championship: Won twice
World Club Challenge: Won once
Premiership: Won twice
Middlesex Sevens: Won once

Challenge Cup: Won twice
Regal Trophy: Won twice
Charity Shield: Won once

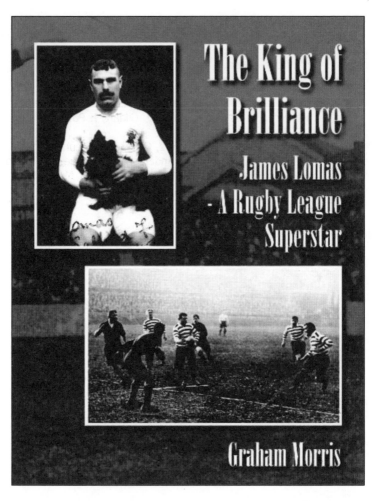

The King of
Brilliance

James Lomas
- A Rugby League
Superstar

Graham Morris

Great new book about one of the sport's genuine legends. James
Lomas played for Bramley, Salford, Oldham and York, and won
representative honours for Lancashire, Cumberland, England and Great
Britain. He captained the first Lions team to tour Australia and New
Zealand in 1910. This is the first biography of him.

Published in October 2011 at £16.95 (hardback).
Signed copies available direct from London League Publications Ltd,
PO Box 65784, London NW2 9NS (cheques payable to London League
Publications Ltd); credit card orders via our website: www.llpshop.co.uk

Two New Zealand rugby legends

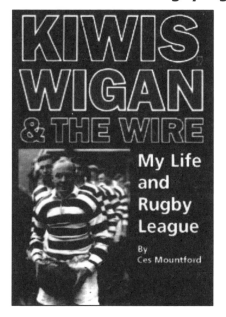

Ces Mountford was a great player for West Coast in New Zealand, and then for Wigan. He then coached Warrington in the 1950s before returning to New Zealand where he became the New Zealand national coach and did great work developing coaching and rugby league in the country.

George Nepia was one of the New Zealand's greatest rugby players. He played rugby union for the All Blacks, and as a 19-year-old was their full-back on their 1924-35 unbeaten tour of Great Britain and France.
In 1935 he switched to rugby league and joined Streatham & Mitcham RLFC in London, and then played for Halifax before returning to New Zealand where he became a dual international by playing for the Kiwis. He was subsequently reinstated into rugby union after the Second World War.

Both books are available direct from London League Publications Ltd for just £5.00 post free in the United Kingdom. Send your order to: LLP, PO Box 65784, London NW2 9NS (cheques payable to London League Publications Ltd); credit card orders via our website: www.llpshop.co.uk

Best in the Northern Union

The pioneering 1910 Rugby League Lions tour of Australia and New Zealand

Tom Mather